America Can Make It!

SENATOR
ABRAHAM RIBICOFF

America
Can Make It!

New York ATHENEUM *1972*

Preface

WHEN Atheneum asked me last spring if I would write a book on some of the great problems confronting this country, I was hesitant to agree. Books by politicians are often only disguised campaign documents read by the faithful few. If the ideas in the book are controversial, the readership may expand slightly to include your opponent in your next election.

Nonetheless, the problems we face kept crossing my path in the Senate, and I decided to take the plunge. A number of issues such as crime, drugs and the war are not discussed in this book. A substantial dialogue already exists in those areas, and I wanted to focus on the tough, basic problems that seem destined to determine the future of this society—and which politicians duck.

No senator could possibly undertake a project like this without the help of a dedicated staff. I have been fortunate in having men and women around me of great ability, and I am grateful to them for their efforts.

February 1972   ABRAHAM RIBICOFF
                                   United States Senate
                                   Washington, D.C.

Contents

Contents

America Can Make It!

I

America's Present Condition

"AMERICA CAN MAKE IT." When I first came to Congress in 1949, that would not have been a startling thesis. But the fashion now is to describe our problems in pessimistic terms and decry our inability and unwillingness to handle them.

Times have changed, and so have we. Once we were a country of eager, confident men and women, sure of our purpose and excited by the challenges of the future. Now we are skeptical about our ability, and the ability of our government, to solve the problems we face.

I found this confirmed in a book which appeared in 1971 entitled *Hopes and Fears of the American People*. It is a study of American attitudes. The volume was researched and written by Albert H. Cantril and Charles W. Roll, Jr., with the Gallup Poll organization. The public was asked if they believed that the unrest and ill feeling between groups in America could lead to a "real breakdown" nationally.

Almost half of those interviewed—47 percent—said they felt national collapse was imminent. The younger the person interviewed, the more likely he or she was to predict breakdown. Young Americans, traditionally the most optimistic group in the nation, today have the least confidence in tomorrow. They and their older countrymen are, to one degree or another, disillusioned.

A popular pastime today is to isolate the causes of the weariness that seems to afflict the American people. Alvin Toffler, in his book *Future Shock,* wrote that events have begun to move faster than our ability to comprehend them. People are torn loose from their accepted values. They are swept along by the tides of change. Margaret Mead noted recently that society is developing so quickly that this is the first generation of parents who have learned from their children. As much information and knowledge has been gained in my lifetime as was gathered in the entire history of mankind.

There is more to our loss of confidence than rapid change and new information. America has been called the land of promise. It could also be called the land of promises. In my thirty-four years in public life, I have heard more promises made for the success of this program and the end of that problem than I can remember. Invariably, the greater the promise of success, the greater the potential for failure. Government failures, unkept promises and deceptions have begun to take their toll on public confidence.

Our involvement in Vietnam has been a sobering, discouraging experience. The war persists even today. No one is sure how we got into it or, with hindsight, what we realistically could have hoped to accomplish. But what we did achieve was monstrous. Fifty-five thousand Americans dead, 300,000 wounded. For what? The government itself has never been able to convince Americans with its answers. The publication of the Pentagon papers only confirmed what more and more Americans already knew —that truth was also a casualty of the Vietnam war. The government deceived the American people and shielded them from the true nature of the conflict.

The Vietnam war was not the first occasion when government misled the people. But Vietnam was unique. It was the first time that so many professional people and political commentators were on the receiving end of so much government propaganda. For the first time, they were led astray on a matter of concern to them. They learned what the poor, the blacks and the unemployed have known for years—that government is what it does, not what it says.

American governments going as far back as Depression times have oversold, overpromoted and overpromised programs. The preambles to almost all of the legislative acts implementing the New Deal asserted that the social problems they dealt with would now be solved once and for all. Year after year, beginning with President Roosevelt, reaching the heights under President Johnson, and continuing with President Nixon, the people of this country have been offered program after program, each with the promise that it was going to end poverty or provide everyone decent housing or guarantee jobs for all or join the races in lives of mutual harmony.

The bureaucrats who administer the programs may believe the slogans. But the people affected by them know better. City dwellers know that urban renewal has created instant slums and saved few cities. Blacks as well as whites know that the problems of racial discord are more intractable today than they were eighteen years ago when the Supreme Court struck down government-sanctioned segregation in the *Brown* v. *Board of Education* decision. Poor people know that welfare programs perpetuate poverty rather than end it. Working families who would like to live in better housing know that federal housing programs have been largely responsible for separating the country into decaying central cities and affluent suburbs. The unskilled unemployed know that most manpower training programs are worthless.

It is time to end this parade of broken promises and frustrated expectations. Our problems are great. But so are the resources of this nation and its people if we can restore their confidence in themselves and their government. The answer is not more or bigger promises. The answer is a willingness on the part of leaders throughout the country to be honest with the American people about the nature of our problems and what we need to do to solve them.

Liberals, in particular, have played a major role in this country's social progress. Liberals therefore have a special duty now to ensure that we do not identify so strongly with the causes and ideas of the past that we forget that time moves on. Too often, political discussions today are little more than a litany of our past theories—theories now woefully out of date.

Those of us who grew up with the New Deal ideology as an article of faith must take a new look at our

7

problems in light of today's conditions and tomorrow's possibilities. What was good twenty years ago may not be good now or for the next twenty years. Where our old theories and programs are no longer valid, we must be willing to reject them. When we are not sure about the answers to a problem, we should say so. And when progress will take time, let us warn people in advance, not discredit whatever progress we make by our own unrealistic promises.

Skepticism about new programs would decrease if we were willing to acknowledge a major failing of politicians as designers of programs: we often sell our ideas without any firm basis on which to hope for success. Few leaders want to document the crisis in health, for instance, and then advocate a small program or a modest first step. The popular response to a huge problem has been a huge program. That is how leaders establish the depth of their commitment.

Huge but unverified programs generate huge hoopla—and huge waste. All the experts in the world cannot predict in advance the impact of a given program on any particular problem in a society as complex as ours. People just do not always respond the way the social scientists predict.

It is time we began to test out our theories and programs before thrusting them full-blown on the country. We should have administered Medicare, for example, for two years on a pilot basis, in, say, ten typical communities across the nation. The lessons we would have learned in demonstration projects would have saved enormous amounts of money and led to needed improvements and reforms before we implemented Medicare on a national basis. Instead, we went full speed ahead immediately. The resulting waste and inflationary costs have led politicians to support cutbacks in the program at a time we should be expanding it, since cutbacks are easier to make than trying to get the bugs out of an unwieldy system.

Another common mistake we make is to design programs for conditions that no longer exist. The facts always seem to be five years ahead of our theories, and our theories are usually five years ahead of our politics. And so we legislate on the basis of theories that are out of date and are based on facts that no longer exist.

By the time the colleges finally provide enough teachers, the number needed for the nation's classrooms has declined, leaving thousands of teachers unemployed. By the time our theory of a general education for everyone is implemented, we find we have made education irrelevant for many who want to learn a trade. And those completing vocational schools find themselves prepared for jobs that existed in 1962.

In addition to being more candid and realistic about our programs, we must also be more persistent. Change and progress take time, and require far more perseverance than we have shown in the past. America is a faddish nation. We move from one issue to another, anxious to be where the action is. For a few years, civil rights was our cause. Then the problems of the cities and poverty moved to the fore. Next it was the Vietnam war, followed by ecology.

Yet poverty is still with us. Discrimination is rampant. The cities are deteriorating. The war continues, and our environment is being polluted. No wonder the average person is skeptical when governments and politicians unveil a new program, saying, "Here's the answer to our newest problem."

Many of the programs and approaches I am discussing in this book will require a great deal of money, in addition to a willingness to see our problems in a new perspective. The legitimate question people should ask is, where is the money coming from in an era of multibillion-dollar deficits? The usual liberal response is to talk about reallocating our priorities to spend less for defense and more for urban problems and to close tax loopholes. I support those general themes. But it's not enough to leave it at that. Given the world as it is, we will have to maintain a credible defense posture. There is no way to fund all our social needs out of military cutbacks.

We must therefore reorder our domestic priorities as well. Some programs are more important than others. Some work better. Unfortunately, the debates rarely get to those issues. Politicians and bureaucrats insist that their own pet programs should be perpetuated. Yes, they have not achieved what we had hoped, they admit. But the missing ingredient always seems to be money. We can no longer afford the luxury of funding programs across the board, thereby doing a little for everything and not much for anything. Too many of our basic social problems are being ignored or tolerated.

Our new domestic priorities must focus on the problems that divide this nation and threaten the fabric that holds our society together: the problems of black and white, rich and poor, the working class and the health of our economy. If politicians ignore these problems, or treat them as just part of a long laundry list, we will fail in our responsibility to solve the basic obstacles to progress in this country.

For politicians, dealing with some of these problems, particularly the question of race, is difficult. When I first came to Washington as a congressman in 1949, Sam Rayburn, the Speaker of the House, spoke to the new group of Democratic members. He gave his famous advice that if we wanted to get along, we should go along. He also noted, "Never make a speech on an issue. You can always explain a vote. But you can never explain a speech." This was good advice for anyone who wants to survive in public office. It was echoed recently in *The Real Majority,* by Richard Scammon and Ben Wattenberg, who cautioned candidates that to win they should seize the middle of the road.

But simply getting along or playing it safe in the middle of the road is no longer sufficient to deal with the great problems we face. Elected officials must also inform and educate the public. We should be in front of the troops, not always behind them, on questions like race and poverty. Unless responsible leaders begin a dialogue on controversial issues, we leave the field by default to crackpots and demagogues.

All of us in public life are fortunate and should be honored to serve in the high, prestigious posts we occupy. All of us would like to continue in those offices. But at the same time, we must be willing to tackle the hardest issues if we are to be worthy of the trust people have placed in us. Playing it safe may win a few more elections, but we could lose a country in the process.

Yes, America can make it. But only if we look at our problems realistically—only if we are honest about the programs we propose to deal with those problems, and only if the President and other elected officials have the vision and courage to be statesmen, willing to take risks and to trust in the inherent decency and common sense of the electorate.

II

School Integration

"HOW CAN A MAN who's supposed to be a liberal like you vote with Senator Stennis on integration?" The young student asking me this question stood belligerently in the aisle of the John F. Kennedy High School auditorium in suburban Plainsville, New York. His chin thrust toward me, his face was grim. It was the first question from the audience of students after my speech about the future role of the United Nations in world affairs.

I looked quickly over the large audience, quiet now, and saw only two black students. I responded,

"I voted with Senator Stennis two months ago so that more than two blacks could sit in this Northern school with 1,000 whites." The students gave me a spontaneous standing ovation.

I have had similar experiences at schools and colleges in this country in the last two years, particularly in the North. Most of these students realized that we have been deceiving ourselves as a nation regarding our goal of integrated schooling for our children. On campus after campus, I have talked to students from the suburbs who lived in all-white neighborhoods and attended all-white schools.

They understand better than most of us that on the subject of school desegregation people do not always mean what they say. We say we are for desegregating schools. But we would prefer to start with the schools across town—or better yet, below the Mason-Dixon Line. There is so much piousness, posturing and clever deception in the debate over desegregation that it is a wonder anyone communicates at all.

On May 17, 1954, the United States Supreme Court ruled that it was unconstitutional for public school systems to willfully segregate students according to race. This was the Court's decision in the *Brown* v. *Board of Education* case. It laid to rest forever the theory that segregated schools could be separate and educate their students equally. Segregated schools were patently unequal, the Court decided. It further asserted that the schools must be desegregated with all deliberate speed. It was a historic decision, a much-needed decision, a big step toward righting past wrongs. But it was not the signal sounding the end of racial segregation in American schools. Much work remained, as we are now finding out.

Many people, however, were confident that with the Supreme Court's decision the nation was on the way toward achieving genuinely integrated schools. Moreover, now that our children would be attending classes together without regard to race, it was felt that they, unlike their parents, would surely grow up free of racial prejudice. They would build, as their elders had failed to build, the open and democratic society we wished to achieve.

Reflective of the mood of the day was this observation about the Court's decision from an article in the *New Republic* of May 31, 1954: "For the 2.5 million Negro children involved it will mean a freshening of the spirit, a liberating sense of their individual value in the American scheme of things. For millions of white children it will mean a chance to grow up without the blinders of racial prejudice and the burden of racial guilt. For the parents of both it will mean an incentive to find new ways of thinking and feeling together. . . . The strait jacket of legal segregation that has confined so many Southern sympathies for so long is about to fall away. We may witness something extraordinary in the way of human growth."

Time and events have shown that this article's enthusiasm was unwarranted. As a nation, we are today, eighteen years later, nowhere near attainment of a racially integrated educational system. The expectations of the fifties were based on hope and good intentions and little else. There was a shortsighted assumption that educational segregation was an isolated occurrence in America. It existed apart from other aspects of our society, and it was most prevalent in the South. Or so the conventional wisdom went.

A fact that today is obvious seems not to have occurred to anybody: that is, that our schools are segregated because our society is segregated. Nor was the point understood that there are more efficient ways to segregate schools than passing laws. In 1954—and for many years thereafter—it was mistakenly believed that in striking down official racial segregation in the schools, the Supreme Court had struck down school segregation itself. That was an illusion, an illusion slow to die.

The Supreme Court said segregated education was

illegal under certain circumstances. But under other conditions, segregation was allowed to continue and grow. It all depended on how a given community's segregation began. If school segregation started with the passage of state and local laws, it was called *de jure* and was ruled unconstitutional. But if the segregation was "accidental"—the result, say, of housing patterns or the racial composition of neighborhoods —then it was termed *de facto* and was legal. This distinction meant that the South, which had passed laws to enforce school segregation, felt the impact of the Court's *Brown* v. *Board of Education* decision. But in the North, where segregation was based not on specific laws but on housing patterns, all-black and all-white schools were left untouched by the Court's decision.

The federal government began using its enforcement power, resources and influence to bring about desegregation of Southern schools. These efforts triggered considerable unrest in the South as resistance, some of it violent, developed. Meanwhile, segregation in Northern schools continued without much federal concern. Not surprisingly, Southern leaders began to object to what they saw as a double standard and demanded that the North be required to desegregate just as the South was. They said it should make no difference what the history of segregation was, whether it was the result of laws or housing patterns. What mattered, they said, was that Southern schools were being pressured to desegregate while Northern schools remained immune from federal integration efforts.

For years these cries of "double standard" were ignored. During the fifties and early sixties, schools were obviously more segregated in the South than in the North. By 1964, for example, less than 2 percent of black students in the deep South attended schools with whites.

After passage of the 1964 Civil Rights Act, the situation began to change. Using the threat of fund cutoffs for federal aid to education, federal agencies began to succeed where the courts had often failed: They began to achieve school integration in the South.

In the North during this same time, the continual migration of whites to the suburbs—the "white flight," as it came to be called—began to aggravate already difficult racial conditions. More and more schools in major central cities such as New York, Detroit and Chicago became all black, and an increasing percentage of black students found themselves in segregated schools.

The trends became clearer in late 1969 when the Department of Health, Education and Welfare published an index of school segregation for the fall of 1968. In numerous Southern states, a substantial majority of black students still attended schools that were virtually 100 percent black. But 18.4 percent of the blacks in the South were in schools with a white majority, a figure that was beginning to rival the Northern figure of 27.6 percent. More interesting to the Southerners were the figures for particular cities. Almost 147,000 black students in New York City, for example, attended schools that were 95 to 100 percent black.

These figures led Senator John Stennis of Mississippi to take up the fight of those arguing that all regions of the country should be treated equally when it came to school segregation. In early 1970 Senator Stennis sought to amend an education bill being debated by the Senate. His proposal, Amendment No. 463, which became known as the Stennis amendment, was simply stated and to the point. The federal government, the amendment said, should promote school desegregation evenly throughout the nation, in the North as well as the South. A key provision called for an end to legal distinctions about segregation of schools. Segregated schools were segregated schools, the amendment asserted. It did not matter what part of the country they were found in or how they got that way.

My instinctive reaction was to oppose the Stennis amendment. I had the greatest respect for John Stennis as a man. But, like many Northerners, I was inclined to ignore anything a Southerner had to say on the subject of integration. We all knew where they stood and therefore paid them little heed.

Senator Stennis had consistently opposed federal civil-rights legislation. His motives in introducing this amendment would surely be questioned. Yet the more I thought about the amendment, the more I came to realize that what the Senator from Mississippi was saying made good sense. What is fair is fair. Regardless of why he introduced the amendment, there was no denying his basic point: if Northern liberals were willing to force the South to desegregate its schools, we should do as much for our own schools, where the problem was becoming increasingly serious.

Without question, many Southerners hoped the Stennis amendment would slow down integration in the South, if only by dissipating federal efforts. Though the Southern states that had dual school systems were desegregating under constitutionally based Supreme Court orders that nobody could change, some hard-core resisters were still trying to circumvent those orders by such methods as segregating classrooms in "integrated" schools or establishing private schools for whites only.

Any kind of slowdown in the South was unaccept-able. But desegregation in the South was not, to my mind, the question in the Stennis amendment. The real question was, how committed were we North-erners to integration in our own backyards? The problem clearly was becoming a national one that demanded a national solution.

I decided to support the Stennis amendment. I had been talking about the problems of segregation in the North in speeches at several colleges and felt an obligation to say in the Senate what I had been saying around the country. Several members of my staff met me at the office on Sunday, February 8, 1970. We worked through the day discussing the amendment and the speech I was going to make. Some suggested the speech talk about the problems in the North without actually supporting Senator Stennis, but I felt this would be inconsistent with what I saw to be the problem.

The next morning, February 9, in my speech in the Senate, I said Northern attitudes toward the South are hypocritical, that we in the North should start practicing at home what we preach to the South. I continued:

The Senator from Mississippi has argued that if segregation is wrong in the public schools of the

22

South, it is wrong in the public schools of all other states. On this statement, the Senator from Mississippi is correct. . . . The North is guilty of monumental hypocrisy in its treatment of the black man. Without question, northern communities have been as systematic and as consistent as Southern communities in denying the black man and his children the opportunities that exist for white people.

The plain fact is that racism is rampant throughout the country. It knows no geographical boundary and has known none since the great migration of rural blacks after World War II.

The institutional roots of racism—which depersonalize our prejudices and make it easier for us to defend them—are as deeply embedded in the large metropolitan communities of the North as they are in the small rural communities of the South.

Perhaps we in the North needed the mirror held up to us by the Senator from Mississippi, in order to see the truth. If Senator John Stennis of Mississippi wants to make honest men of Northern liberals, I think we should help him. But first, we must be honest with ourselves.

Our problem is not only the dual systems of education which exist sixteen years after the Supreme Court struck them down in 1954.

The more fundamental problem is the dual society that exists in every metropolitan area—the black society of the central city and the white society

23

of the suburb.

Massive school segregation does not exist because we have segregated our schools but because we
have segregated our society. . . .

My speech and the fact that I had sided with a
Southern senator on a racial issue provoked wide-
spread comment and criticism. Roy Wilkins, president of the National Association for the Advance-
ment of Colored People (NAACP), said: "It is sad
to report that the former Governor of Connecticut,
Senator Ribicoff, beat the White House for the honor
of endorsing the raping of equality in education." An
NAACP newsletter was distributed in my state of
Connecticut, declaring: "The bigoted, conservative
Southern whites . . . continue to be our enemies.
. . . And they've got helpers like Senator Abraham Ribicoff."

Tom Wicker in a New York *Times* column head-
lined "The Death of Integration" wrote: "Poor old
Union! Its great and generous dreams falling one by
one to a dusty death." Editorially, the *Times* described the Stennis amendment as an effort to "convert liberal guilt into segregationist glee." In the
Washington *Post,* David S. Broder thought I had
"progressed in only 10 years from being John Kennedy's favorite governor to being John Stennis's favorite Senator." Mr. Broder also announced the

"death of the American dream" was upon us, in large measure, he said, due to the Stennis amendment.

Over at the Washington *Star,* an editorial explained my behavior by suggesting Senator Ribicoff had "lost his sense of direction" and at *The Nation* it was felt that I had joined the Stennis amendment in a "moment of bemusement." Columnist Carl Rowan was certain I had been "duped" by Senator Stennis into signing on with a "nationwide alliance of segregationists." An editorial in the *Wall Street Journal* warned that a "considerable potential for mischief lurks in Senator Ribicoff's curious alliance with Senator Stennis."

In making those Senate remarks—and in allying myself on this issue with a Southerner—I did not intend to betray the civil-rights movement, allow myself to be duped, lose my direction, register a setback to integration or deflate the American dream. I did intend to prod all Americans, from all parts of the nation, into a recognition that school segregation is a national problem and must be dealt with accordingly.

Unfortunately, few Northern liberals were willing to join me in this effort. They argued that the problem was still more severe in the South and we should focus our efforts there. They objected to the fact that the Stennis amendment was only a statement of principle and contained no program. And they sharply questioned Senator Stennis's motives in putting this amendment forward.

Nonetheless, the amendment passed, 56 to 36, only to be watered down by the Senate-House conference. But the important point had been made. It was that the North and the South both have segregated schools and that efforts to desegregate must be national in scope and uniform in application.

Incidentally, I do not think it immodest to say that had I not supported the Stennis amendment it would never have passed. Nor would it have provoked the lively debate it did. But the catalyst was not I, personally. It was what I represented. It was that a senator from the North with liberal credentials actually listened to a Southerner and took him seriously on an issue affecting the races. Any liberal senator speaking out in favor of the Stennis amendment would have set off the controversy that followed. It is a sad commentary on the diversity of political dialogue in this nation that most white Southerners have been, by circumstance or choice, largely excluded from serious debate about racial issues.

Two key actions were taken directly as a result of the Senate's passage of the Stennis amendment. Following the debate and vote, the Senate established a Select Committee on Equal Educational Opportunity at the urging of Senator Walter F. Mondale, of Minnesota, a brilliant young senator dedicated to the cause of civil rights. Then the Nixon administration responded by proposing several weeks later that financial assistance be given to those schools desegregating under administrative or court order.

Neither of these two developments went anywhere immediately, however. The Select Committee, unfortunately, got off on the wrong foot, to begin with. The committee was supposed to develop programs for breaking down segregation in Northern schools, but spent the first six months of its existence probing segregation in the schools of the South. Only then did it turn to the difficult problems confronting the North. The President's $1.5 billion Emergency School Aid Act of 1970, aimed at helping school districts desegregate, passed in the House but did not pass in the Senate before adjournment.

Further proof—if new proof were needed—of my contention that the North was hypocritical toward the South on segregated schools was seen on November 4, 1971, when political panic swept the House of Representatives as it voted, 231 to 126, to prohibit the use of federal dollars to help school systems achieve racial balance with busing. Many Northern liberal congressmen voted against busing, and many more liberals avoided the issue by not voting. When busing was being used almost exclusively in the South to achieve racial balance, congressional opposition was not heavy. But when the issue came home, when programs were put forward to integrate a few Northern schools with busing, Northern liberals joined with conservatives and others to cut off federal funds for such projects.

The sad irony is that many of these Northerners, as well as Southerners, were voting against the interests of their constituents. The House vote did not rescind the court orders for busing. No House or Senate vote can do that. All the House did in its uncritical response to what has become a political scare word was deny funds to those schools that are now or will soon be engaged in busing programs.

Some spokesmen representing the Northern point of view have continued to say that there is a decided difference between the segregation of the South (*de jure*) and that of the North (*de facto*). *De facto* segregation can only be fought in the courts, the argument goes. During the debate on the Stennis amendment several senators from Northern states said there was nothing Congress could do about integrating Northern schools until the Supreme Court took the lead and ruled against neighborhood, or *de facto*, segregation.

I disagreed then and continue to do so now. That

position reverses the constitutional role of the Supreme Court. The Court is to function as an arbiter of last resort. The Court was never meant to be the first to enter the fray. The highest tribunal was to act when all other avenues of redress had been tried and found wanting. The Court wisely moved against law-imposed, or *de jure,* segregation in 1954 because neither the Congress nor the executive branch nor the states and school districts had done what needed to be done.

To drop the question of *de facto,* or Northern, school segregation at the steps of the Supreme Court is to duck the issue, particularly at this time in our history when the nation is in need of responsible, constructive leadership from its elected officials. If the President and the Congress continue to abdicate their constitutional responsibilities, then they will force the courts—and ultimately the Supreme Court —to try to assume the entire burden themselves.

Regrettably, the courts are not equipped to implement successfully programs to bring about desegregation nationwide. Court litigation costs are high. Issues must be tried in courtroom after courtroom, in city after city, with each case being judged individually. These cases are frequently long and drawn-out. Then, once decisions are handed down, the courts are unable to provide the money to implement their decrees. Finally, court litigation requires adversary proceedings, with someone being found "guilty" of racism, overt discrimination or illegal and unconstitutional actions. Ultimately, a scapegoat is found. To others he may be a hero. Confrontations develop. Communities tend to polarize. Moderates on both sides are forced into more extreme positions. The problem may become worse as months and years drag by.

In addition, years of litigation will only establish that there is no real distinction between law-imposed, *de jure*, segregation (Southern style) and neighborhood-imposed, *de facto*, segregation (the Northern version). I am confident that if we want to spend the time, money and resources litigating the issue of segregation in the North, jurists will establish that certain school districting and zoning decisions, the drafting of building codes, municipal housing policies, the locating of certain schools and other official actions were purposefully formulated to separate the races residentially as well as educationally. Cases in Richmond, Virginia, in Pasadena, California, and in Pontiac and Detroit, Michigan, have already moved in this direction. But once we have repeated this process across the country, what will we have done to improve a situation we all know exists and should deplore? There is enough responsibility and guilt to go around. How much more time do we have to waste and how many more cases do we have to litigate before we have proved the point?

We would be better advised now to acknowledge that there is a critical problem facing this country—North and South—and to then devote our energies to solving that problem. There is little to be gained by arguing who is to blame. A guilty conscience or a criminal penalty never taught a youngster how to read.

Yet the same old tired debate goes on. We can debate the relative evils of *de jure* and *de facto* segregation indefinitely. But for the black child who is forced to suffer a segregated education, the argument —the distinction between *de facto* and *de jure*—is meaningless. No matter what it is called, or how it got there, it is still segregation. To the black child, it means that white people don't think his life is as important as their children's and that he is not good enough to associate with their youngsters.

How the child learns this lesson, whether in an all-black *de jure* or *de facto* classroom, is not important. The point is he gets the message, loud and clear. The damage can be permanent. It can affect the black child for the rest of his life. No legal phrase can soften the blow or ease the pain. The phrase *de facto* does serve a purpose, however. It provides a "respectable" screen behind which white Americans can discriminate against black children.

The irony in all of the recent posturing by Northerners is that today the South's schools are more integrated than are the North's. Since the Senate debate on the Stennis amendment, new figures have conclusively demonstrated that the problem of school segregation is now more Northern than Southern. From 1968 to 1971, the percentage of blacks in Southern states attending majority white schools increased from 18.4 percent to 43.9 percent. In the North, the figures remained almost constant, moving from 27.6 percent to 27.8 percent.

Even more ominously, the 1970 census data, released after the Stennis debate, demonstrate that the South is now urbanizing along Northern lines: central cities are becoming blacker and the suburbs will soon be just as white. Atlanta's central-city population went from 38.3 percent black in 1960 to 51.3 percent black in 1970, while its suburbs went from 91.3 percent white to 93.6 percent white. Houston's suburbs by 1970 were 90.7 percent white, and New Orleans' were 87.2 percent white.

In time, therefore, Southern leaders will argue that *de jure* segregation is gone. In its place will be the Northern-style *de facto* segregation. As proof, the South will soon be able to say its cities and suburbs are just like the North's—black cities, white suburbs. What an unlikely turnabout that the model for segregation should come from the North. For so many years, we labored under the illusion that racial discrimination emanated exclusively from the South, where the legacy of slavery and legalized segregation was responsible for most of the race tension in the nation.

There is little doubt that if life had been better in the South, blacks would have remained there and not embarked on the migration north. But when the blacks moved north they were greeted by ghettos, unemployment lines, slums, poor schools and inadequate medical care. All our criticism of the South, no matter how justified, cannot excuse or erase these facts. The North has been just as successful in denying to the black man and his family the opportunities we insist upon for ourselves and our families.

We tell ourselves that it isn't our fault. The institutions are responsible. There is nothing we can do. It all happened accidentally. That being said, another disclaimer must be made. It is that the "accident" theory isn't good enough any more. How blacks ended up this way is no longer of any consequence. We have studied the problem to death. We should forget yesterday and concern ourselves with today and tomorrow.

Where do we start? We begin by recognizing that we don't have to wait for the Supreme Court to rule on *de facto* segregation. The President and the Congress have all the power they need.

We must also see the problem of school desegregation for what it is—not what we would like it to be. We need to recognize the fact that our present efforts to desegregate our schools are failing and will continue to fail. In many communities, the desegregation effort has fanned old hatreds and created new ones. The effort—admittedly in pursuit of a noble goal—has made matters worse in some areas. Focusing on integration in our central cities has driven many of the remaining white families to the sanctuary of the surrounding suburbs. In city after city we have integrated our schools only to find that the entire city has become segregated. Washington's 94 percent black central-city school population is only the harbinger of things to come in public education.

It is time we tried a new approach, an approach based on fairness, realism and universal applicability. We should set realistic goals and learn from the lessons of the past eighteen years, not charge blindly on, doomed to repeat earlier mistakes. Until we make a true assessment of this situation, we cannot expect to improve it.

For a starter, I want to propose a twelve-year program. Long-range programs for integration have been discredited because they became the last bastion of Southern segregationists after eight to ten years of refusal to integrate at all. But it is instructive to remember that had we begun school integration in the South one grade at a time, all the schools of the South would have been desegregated in twelve years. Instead, it was twelve years before we saw the first signs of any significant progress.

Which will it be, we must ask ourselves, the "All or Nothing at All" lyric of everything or nothing, or an approach of sure, genuine progress? We can insist on having the best of all possible worlds overnight—and not get it—or we can proceed one step at a time, secure in the knowledge that we are moving forward, that we will have better schools this year than last and that with each new school term our goal of a just and realistic racial balance within our schools will be that much closer.

Desegregation—in the South and North—is a major undertaking. It is not the sort of social change that can simply be imposed by a court and implemented from Washington—unless the people affected by it, both white and black, are in some sympathy with it. It has taken us eighteen years to learn that we cannot force white parents to send their children to school with black children without some semblance of community support for the effort. Yes; it can be done—but at what price? Community strife, bitterness, recriminations, polarization, cynicism and the continuing flight of the whites. That is the price we pay. It is a price we should not have to pay.

To begin with, force should never have become a factor. We failed in our very terminology. "Forced integration," "forced busing," "forced low-cost housing in the suburbs," forced anything—these are scare words to the American people and they will react adversely to them every time. We demanded too much too soon, and when we got too little the courts moved in and began ordering almost overnight desegregation plans that very few people approved of or would support.

In the face of the magnitude of the problem confronting us now in the North as well as in the South, the temptation today is to give up and go on to something else. The "radical chic" position occupied by a handful of black militants arguing for separation has led many to ask, "Why should we fight for integration when many blacks themselves call for separatism?" It is true that some blacks don't want integration. And whenever a black man says this, you can almost hear the sigh of relief rising from the white suburbs.

White tokenism in both the North and the South

has made some blacks frustrated, bitter and angry. They want only to be left alone. But it's a curious kind of morality that drives blacks to such despair over the possibilities of achieving integration and then uses this despair to justify doing—or not doing —what we have always done or not done.

The most important fact is this: Most blacks still favor integration. A study of almost 3,000 blacks in fifteen major cities was done in 1968 by Angus Campbell and Howard Schuman of the Survey Research Center. They found that less than 15 percent of the blacks interviewed supported separate black neighborhoods, 48 percent strongly supported integrated neighborhoods and another 37 percent had no strong preference either way.

This and other studies have shown that most blacks cling to the same hopes and goals America has held out to every other group. Denying them their rightful opportunity because a minority of blacks has become impatient is a shabby betrayal of the ideals this country is supposed to represent.

Similarly, it is too easy to argue that the cause is hopeless because Americans at heart are racists who, given their way, will consign blacks forever to a separate and inferior status in society. This convenient myth is not supported by the facts. Public opinion polls show that most Americans favor integration and are willing to send their children to desegregated schools. Substantial opposition to integration generally occurs only when schools and neighborhoods cease to reflect the racial composition of the society at large.

In May 1970, the Gallup Poll reported that only 6 percent of Northern parents and 10 percent of Southern parents would object to sending their children to a school where there were "a few" blacks. (This was a drop from 61 percent in the South only seven years earlier.) The percentages objecting increased to 24 percent in the North and 43 percent in the South when half the student body was to be black. And, if a majority of the students were to be black, objections were rendered by 51 percent of Northern parents and 69 percent of Southern parents. The National Opinion Research Center reported in December 1971 that over half the whites in the South favored integrated schools while the percentage among whites nationally was 75 percent in favor. The authors noted that this was after the great publicity given to recent riots, black separatism and urban crime.

White opposition to sending their children to majority black schools need not present an insurmountable problem if we view the entire metropolitan area—including the suburbs—as a whole. The percentage of blacks living in most of these areas is less than 20 percent. In fact, in the major metropolitan areas in 1970, blacks made up only 12 percent of the population.

But this is a figure virtually unknown in the heated, acrimonious debate now surrounding integration. Words take on a meaning of their own. Because we crowded blacks into small land areas within our cities, integrated schools soon became stereotyped as predominantly black schools. To make matters worse, they also became synonymous with inferior if not outright useless schools.

Ask the average American about sending his child to an integrated school and ironically he now assumes you are talking about a segregated school— that is, one that's mostly black. And yet, in Hartford, Connecticut, where the metropolitan area contains a school population only 12 percent black, it is obviously physically impossible to make every school or even a large number of schools predominantly black. If we look at the entire metropolitan area, we find that there simply aren't that many blacks.

We are now in the process of debasing the language even further. Integration will soon, given the lack of leadership on this issue, be synonymous with that great scare word "busing." If we had trouble gaining support in the white community for integrated schools when everyone assumed they would be lousy and all black, imagine the response as those whites also assume that busing means their children will be transported fifty miles each way to attend that "integrated" school.

Yet, as too few note, millions of American children already are bused to school, and no one is objecting. State and federal education officials estimate that as many as two-thirds of all school children—some 30 million children—ride buses to school each day. Suburban parents often insist upon the opportunity for their children to ride on a school bus as a matter of right.

The greatest irony is that a recent study in *South Today,* published by the Southern Regional Council in Atlanta, found that students attending private white "academies" in the South are being bused up to 120 miles a day. Bused pupils for the ten segregated private schools studied in eight states were found to travel an average of 7.6 miles farther each way to and from school than pupils bused to public schools in those states. Perhaps the buses used to achieve racial imbalance offer a more enjoyable ride than those used to end segregation.

Busing is only one technique for integrating schools. Many school districts have successfully integrated their schools by redrawing district lines, pairing neighborhood schools and locating new schools in areas that make integration easier. These techniques have actually reduced the amount of busing in some areas.

Many who object to busing don't really object to the bus ride. Their concern is the school at the end of the ride. As long as broad disparities exist in the caliber of students, teachers, atmosphere and equipment in our schools, parents have every right to be concerned over proposals to take their children from schools they know to facilities unknown to them. America cannot allow these disparities in its schools to continue. But the solution is not continued opposition to integration. Nor can we limit our efforts only to improving ghetto schools. Integration and the improvement of all schools must go forward together.

With or without busing, lasting school integration cannot occur in a segregated society. It is a fantasy to think that integration can be achieved by letting black children attend our schools when we won't let them live in our neighborhoods. We must recognize once and for all that we cannot require the schools to bear the entire brunt of our attempts to integrate our society. For years we have incorrectly assumed that integrated education would lead to an integrated society. Figures in the South dispel that notion. They show that today, while educational integration is increasing, residential segregation is also on the rise.

If these trends continue, we will soon be confronted in the South and throughout this nation with the situation we have in Washington, D.C. Talk about integrating central-city schools is an academic exercise in the nation's capital, where the school population is 94 percent black.

Integrated education is our goal. But unless we open the suburbs to those trapped in the city, we will labor in vain. That is why I have proposed two programs at the federal level. The first would require gradual but real integration in all our major metropolitan area schools. The second would place the force of the federal government behind efforts to open the suburbs to housing for low- and moderate-income families. The second proposal is discussed further in chapters III and IV.

The first measure—the Urban Education Improvement Act of 1971—requires state and local educational agencies in metropolitan areas throughout the country to develop and implement plans to reduce and eliminate minority-group isolation in the public schools no matter what the cause of that isolation. The *de jure–de facto* argument would be silenced for good.

Federal financial assistance would be granted for the development and implementation of these plans. Variations would be allowed to meet local conditions and needs. But each plan would have to provide that within twelve years every school in the metropolitan area would have a percentage of minority-group students equal to at least half the percentage of minority-group students in the metropolitan area as a whole.

For example, as noted, the percentage of minority-group children in Hartford, the capital city of my own state of Connecticut, and its metropolitan area is about 12 percent black and 4 percent Spanish-speaking. The Hartford central-city percentages are 48 and 18, respectively, for a total minority-group percentage of 66 percent. Under my proposal, the Hartford area schools would have a total minority-group population of at least 8 percent no later than twelve years after adoption of an acceptable plan. Progress would have to be shown each year. Noncooperating school districts would not receive federal education funds and states that funded such noncooperating districts would lose federal funds for state-wide programs.

This bill is designed to learn from the lessons of the last eighteen years. It is clear that we must offer incentives and assistance to those who undertake new challenges. We cannot reasonably expect state and local educational agencies to fund new programs out of existing, often inadequate budgets. In addition, we must give people time to work out their own programs and they must be confident their schools will reflect the racial composition typical of the society at large.

While we seek to end racial desegregation as soon as possible, we must realize that our goal cannot be achieved immediately. My legislation includes provision for a two-year planning period before a ten-year implementation period, to enable us to gain experience at the local and national levels regarding the best methods for dealing with the relationships of the suburbs and the cities.

The measure also leaves the selection of techniques to be used to achieve desegregation to the local educational agencies of the metropolitan area. A number of possible techniques are identified in my bill, including construction of magnet schools and educational parks together with school redistricting, pairing and busing. But it should be clear that this bill is not simply or primarily a busing bill. Transportation is identified as a useful technique in an overall program. But if we have to depend solely upon busing children from one area to another on a metropolitan-wide basis to achieve integration, we will fail no matter what plan we adopt. Success will come only if we open up the suburbs for housing as well as education, for we will never have truly integrated schools until we have an integrated society. Schools have faced the challenge of integration by themselves too long.

I cannot believe that massive opposition to this legislation will arise. I cannot believe that the basic decency of the American people would allow them to resist having a minimum of two or three black and Spanish-speaking students in a class of thirty, as would be required in areas like Hartford, Connecticut. Even in the most heavily black metropolitan areas such as Baltimore, where 32 percent of the students in the metropolitan area are black, we are only talking about each class having at least 16 percent of its students black at the end of twelve years. This is four or five blacks in each class. These figures make it clear that only when we promote school integration throughout our metropolitan areas can we guarantee sufficient stability to avoid the white flight that has characterized large-scale integration thus far.

Nonetheless, even with this approach, it is not clear that the Congress is prepared to move forward in this area. In the spring of 1971, I tried in the Senate to add my legislation to the President's proposal to provide funds to schools integrating under court or federal government order. I applauded his action to provide such assistance for the first time to hard-pressed schools. But I argued that this would not move us forward beyond the area of court-ordered integration. I noted that I would support the Stennis amendment again, for the intervening months had only made it clearer than ever that segregation is a national rather than a regional problem.

To their credit, some of those who criticized me a year earlier were now willing to support this effort. Tom Wicker's column now was headed, "Mr. Ribicoff Comes Through." Stewart Alsop called it "Ribicoff's revenge." And David Broder graciously wrote: "Many of us—this columnist included—were critical of Ribicoff, thinking that he was, for whatever reason, playing the Southern diehard's game. That judgment, it now appears, was overhasty and wrong."

Senator Walter Mondale courageously volunteered to be a cosponsor of my bills and worked vigorously for passage of my school legislation. He noted that his months of hearings with the Senate Select Subcommittee on Equal Education had demonstrated that a metropolitan approach was the only possible solution.

Tom Wicker wrote that it would be interesting to see how many of those Southerners and the few liberals who supported my stand a year earlier on the Stennis amendment would have the "courage" to join me now. I was interested too. After the Stennis amendment debate a year earlier, I had harbored the dream—or hope—that a way could be found to work out a solution to this problem that, for the first time, liberals and Southerners could both support. I had thought that the fantasy was to imagine Southerners voting for an integration bill. It never occurred to me that Northerners would be the ones to back off at the last moment.

I was wrong. After a long, often heated debate, the Senate voted against my amendment, 51 to 35. Eight Southerners, including Senator Stennis, Senator William Fulbright, Senator Howard Baker and Senator John Sherman Cooper, voted with me, as did all the Democratic presidential candidates at the time. But as David Broder noted, the "unlikely comrades" of the Nixon administration and the NAACP worked against the bill and they were joined by eighteen senators who would generally be thought of as liberals on the question of integration. They had all sorts of reasons. Let's not be hasty, they said, we've got to go slow. In fact, most of the opposing arguments had been rejected out of hand when offered by Southerners in years gone by. Moreover, the legislation in question was drafted with many of these points in mind.

Since the spring of 1971, the situation has deteriorated even further. Liberals in the Senate as well as the House have begun to develop "compromises" on the question of school busing rather than deal directly with the fears and myths surrounding this question. In the face of pressure in the presidential primaries from Governor George Wallace, Senator Hubert Humphrey and Senator Henry Jackson changed their positions and opposed my education proposal when it came to a vote again in the Senate in February 1972, losing 65 to 29. And, as I correct page proofs, President Nixon has just signaled to the country an officially sanctioned retreat to the "separate—but equal" school doctrine discredited by the Supreme Court in 1954.

We are clearly at a turning point in the drive for national unity and equality. The limited progress we have made in two decades toward building a unified society is threatened and may already be at an end. President Nixon and the Congress have failed in a time of crisis to provide any positive leadership to develop programs to unite this country. In fact, the President is now leading the way toward total racial apartheid in this country.

America is never going to make it with leadership like this. If Abraham Lincoln was correct over a hundred years ago when he warned that this nation could not survive half-slave and half-free, it is equally clear that we cannot endure if we permit the formation of separate black and white societies that communicate with each other by sending ambassadors across boundaries of hate and fear.

III

Housing—the Problems

A HOME IS NOT a house only. It is a front yard and back, a neighborhood and neighbors, reasonably easy access to work and play, schools, shopping centers, entertainment, restaurants and health care. A home is a family's image onto the world, a big investment—the biggest investment many couples ever make—a source of comfort and security, a sanctuary for privacy and thought. One of this nation's basic principles is that every American should have the right to buy or rent a home with all that and anything more he or she wishes to make of it. But millions of

Americans do not have that opportunity. They are forced to live in either housing they deplore or neighborhoods they would like to avoid.

There is more to housing than buildings. Housing is where we as a people live and how we live and with whom we associate. It is what use we make of land and how we distribute our resources. If in our housing we separate ourselves, then we separate ourselves as a people as well. That is why this chapter and the one that follows are not only about a failure of housing policy and programs. They are about more. For we are now confronted with the potential destruction of the fabric that has held together the various segments of our society.

Present patterns of urban, suburban and rural development show the potential for the rupturing of this nation along economic, social and racial lines. The affluent are moving farther and farther away from the poor and the black. Historically, the egalitarian melting-pot theory of our society has often been more romantic fiction than fact. When viewed as an absolute—a society in which all differences among people are unnoticed—the melting pot was mostly unreal. But when seen as a mixture that allows many people of many backgrounds to come together to work and live within a democratic framework, the melting-pot image of America has been valid to a large degree.

It is true that ethnic groups and recent immigrants frequently clustered together out of common bonds of heritage, language and family. But it is also true that assimilation has generally always been possible and even when not taking place the separation between the haves and the have-nots was once only a matter of a few blocks or a short trip across the tracks. Our communities, rural and urban, in the past contained within themselves racial, social and economic variety and contact.

I am reminded of the New Britain, Connecticut, of my youth. It was a city of heavy industry and high hopes. People of all races, colors and creeds had come there because of the opportunity for jobs and a better way of life. The New Britains of America gave birth to the melting-pot theory and, as I have defined it, the theory was valid. Men, women and children had come to New Britain from all parts of the world to progress and build new lives for themselves. My parents arrived in 1909 from Poland. I was born a year later.

Perhaps because there was so much diversity, the outward differences that divide people—race, color, and creed—were not so important. Tolerance was encouraged. There was only one high school, for instance, and virtually everybody who went to high school attended New Britain High. The brotherhood of man was not a concept we concerned ourselves with very much, I must admit. But there was a willingness to accept one another for our deeds and how we conducted ourselves. And there was a mutual respect among families, even between those whose backgrounds and habits were totally different. There may not have been much love lost between us. But there was tolerance and mutual respect.

Today life in America is changing. The society is splitting up into social, economic and racial enclaves. Groups are adopting symbols and mannerisms that may be based on ethnic and regional pride but that have the added result of irritating and annoying and hurting other groups. There is little mutual respect and tolerance any more. Yet never in my life have I heard so much talk of love. Forgive my nostalgia, but I'll take the good old days where people may not have particularly liked each other, but at least they recognized each other as human beings. They had real, face-to-face contact with each other. Their impressions of one another were not based on imaginary fears and suspicions.

It is different today. Those we fear and suspect most we may never see, let alone speak with. The often arbitrary municipal boundary between suburbs and central city—and between suburb and suburb—

serves as a wall not to be breached or surmounted. Affluent families have carved out their own "turf" and outsiders are not welcome. All our housing problems are not the result of the suburbs by any means. But much of what has happened to us as a people has happened in concert with the growth of suburban living. We are, more than anything else, a suburban nation.

In 1940, suburbs contained 27 million people; two out of every ten Americans; 19 million fewer than the cities. The 1970 census reveals how times have changed. Today 76 million people live in the suburbs. That is nearly four in every ten Americans. Twelve million more people live in the suburbs than the central cities. The suburbs are 95 percent white. During the last ten years alone, central cities have lost 2.5 million whites and gained 3 million blacks. The sixty-six largest metropolitan area suburbs gained 12.5 million whites and only 760,000 blacks during that same period. As discussed in the preceding chapter, this phenomenon is taking place in the South as well as the North. We can soon expect every major metropolitan area of this country to be composed of a predominantly black central city surrounded by basically white suburbs.

By 1990, 200 million people will live in the metropolitan areas of this country, three-fourths of the en-

tire U.S. population. Most of this additional growth
—50 million more people—will take place in the
suburbs. This growth has occurred at the expense of
the central cities. The city's own image of itself has
been destroyed. The concept of the city as the center
—as the hub of economic and cultural action—is no
longer valid.

What was once a financial pinch for cities now approaches financial strangulation. Funds from almost
all sources are slowing down or drying up. Increased
needs and inflation are pushing costs steadily higher.
Some observers foresee widespread bankruptcy in
the big cities. The middle class, once the strength of
the city, has left for the suburbs. Often the former
city dweller who moves to the suburbs loses interest
in urban problems. Suburban residents frequently are
apathetic or hostile to the problems of the working
class, the elderly, the black, the poor and others
whom they left behind. But, as Baltimore city plan-
ner Larry Reich said, "The City of Baltimore makes
[its] suburbs possible because we carry the burdens
of the old, poor, black. . . . Why should we keep
carrying the burden?"

Financially and demographically, the picture is
disturbing. But more is involved than simply a question of who lives where. As the distance separating
the economic classes and the races grows greater,

fears, suspicions, myths and hatreds increase as well. Our greatest fears are of the unknown and we are developing masses of people in this country who don't know one another. The stories are legion of middle-class students graduating from suburban high schools without ever once visiting downtown or talking to a black or a poor person from the central city. This lack of communication only fosters and heightens misunderstandings and suspicions and the stereotypes of life so many now cling to with the grip of desperation.

Ironically, the suspicion and fear are most widespread where we would least expect to find them. We find that the farther people live from the central city, for example, the more likely they are to be deeply concerned about crime. A 1969 Harris poll showed that many persons' fear of crime is exaggerated. Proportionate to the amount of crime in their area, the people least in danger—those who live in the safest areas of the cities and suburbs—are the most afraid. In such areas, the odds of being robbed may be 1 in 300. In high-crime areas the odds for a resident are 1 in 50. If fear corresponded to fact, residents of high-crime areas should be six times more concerned than those in low-crime areas. In fact, the poll revealed, they are only half as afraid.

Another indication of inflated fear in safer areas is

the professed firsthand knowledge of crime. Though burglary is three times more frequent in high-crime areas, a larger percentage of residents in low-crime areas claim they know burglary victims. The disparity is even more marked between college-educated persons, 70 percent of whom say they know a victim, and those with an eighth-grade education, of whom only 29 percent say they know a victim. Since college graduates generally earn more and live in safer areas, how is it that 41 percent more of them know burglary victims?

This wide gap in perceptions may help to explain another major finding of the Harris poll. That was the sharp differences in attitudes about the causes of crime and what to do to control it. People who live in the central city and who see crime often and at first hand put far heavier emphasis on practical, specific causes such as drug addiction and unemployment. But residents from low-crime areas tend to stress quite different factors like Supreme Court decisions and lack of parental discipline. In general, the poll underscored the conclusion that the image of crime in the minds of the affluent is more vivid than the reality of crime for those who live in central cities.

In their fear, suburban communities are going to considerable lengths in meeting the threat, be it imagined or real, of crime. The ultimate strategy is seen in new housing developments in California and Florida where island communities are surrounded by a moat next to a golf course. Instead of preserving ancient manuscripts as was done in the Dark Ages, it is more likely the cherished items in these fortresses are Martini olives, matched golf clubs and the other artifacts of this growing suburban subculture.

House Beautiful magazine also reported on housing developments designed to prevent crime. Outside Houston, Texas, families are moving into Sugar Creek, a thousand-acre subdivision of $50,000 to $250,000 single-family homes. Sugar Creek has been called "the first walled city in the U.S." A six-foot masonry wall surrounds the area. The only two entrances are guarded twenty-four hours a day and every house is fitted with electronic alarm devices. When they are tripped, bells ring, lights go on and private police are dispatched to the scene.

In Palm Springs, a luxury condominium known as Mission Hills offers buyers one of the first Westinghouse electronic security systems. Electronic sensors in each home are tied to alarms and a master control panel. Computer tape flows from the panel, pinpointing an emergency. The panel is manned by a franchised agency of Westinghouse from which men are sent to help.

By these illustrations, I do not mean to minimize

the threat of crime in more affluent neighborhoods. The danger may, indeed, be genuine. However, there is another danger in all this that is equally threatening. It is that in seeking to isolate, if not simply protect, themselves from the cities, the suburbs will begin to resemble those very evils they perceive in the cities. Putting forth the maxim that "we become what we hate," Irish writer George William Russell has suggested that "by intensity of hatred nations create in themselves the characters they imagine in their enemies. Hence it is that all passionate conflicts result in the interchange of characteristics."

The same holds true for individuals and groups. A suburb surrounded by a moat and high walls, its homes and apartments wired for intruders, defended by a private police force always at the ready, is a suburb obsessed and dominated by crime—although not a single crime need ever be committed. Never have FDR's words, that we have nothing to fear but fear itself, been more meaningful. A terrified community, no matter how rich and prosperous, is not a happy community.

None of the precautions work anyway. No matter how high the fence, the suburbs are finding all over America that they cannot completely insulate themselves from the problems of the central city. Crime, drugs and poverty all slowly find their way to the suburbs as well. The *Wall Street Journal* ran an article on December 23, 1971, entitled "Shoplifting, Long a Plague of Urban Stores, Is Now an Increasing Menace in the Suburbs." Census Bureau figures reveal that the suburbs accounted for half of 1970's increase in this country's poverty population. All that is accomplished by our frantic efforts to insulate ourselves is the polarization of large elements of society.

As the suburbs arm themselves, so do the cities divide up into armed camps. As Stewart Alsop reported from Newark a year ago, this tense New Jersey city has taken sides, the white ethnics rallying behind Tony Imperiale, head of the North Ward Citizens Committee; the blacks under the banner of Sheik Kamiel Wadud, a Black Muslim leader. In a chilling article about Newark, Alsop wrote that Imperiale and Wadud have bands of tough, angry men under their commands. But their armies are not necessarily preparing to battle each other. Suspicious of one another they may be, Mr. Alsop reported, but they have a common enemy—the suburbs.

The real cause of the trouble, Imperiale said, is that there is a "dual system—one set of rules for the blacks, another for us." Who makes the rules? "People who live in ivory towers," Imperiale answered. "People who live on terrain where I and the blacks can't live." Sheik Wadud was of a similar mind, as he observed, "Sure, everybody's got a little venom in them. But against who? Not against the Italian people. Not against the black people. Against the people who don't let us share in the booty. We've fought in every war, but we never got our share of the booty." To that, Imperiale added his prediction that in the next round of urban riots blacks will move against the suburbs, attack utilities and water supplies and "cover the highways with sniper fire."

Against this backdrop, Newark's black Mayor Kenneth Gibson noted that "wherever the cities are going, Newark is going to get there first." I hope the Mayor's remarks are wrong as applied to the Tony Imperiales and Sheik Waduds of Newark. But what if they are right? What if soon all our cities begin dividing up into angry ethnic groups who have but one thing in common—a hatred for the suburbs? Word of these city coalitions can, of course, lead the suburbs to demand more defenses against city encroachments. Or they can lead us to renewed determination to halt the momentum toward warring camps glaring at each other over zoning laws and city lines.

We will need more than reports and rhetoric to make any progress in this area. Too many of our discussions about issues—no matter how specific the question—have degenerated into rhetorical contests to see who can assume the correct posture the fastest.

One example of this occurred recently in the furor surrounding the city of New York's proposal to build a low-income housing project in the middle-class neighborhood of Forest Hills. The facts soon lost out completely.

It now seems clear that city officials failed in their efforts to discuss adequately the location of three twenty-four-story buildings in Forest Hills with those most involved—the residents of Forest Hills. The lack of communication between the city and the residents started rumors flying as fast as words could be uttered. Rumors soon become fact and everyone assumed that thousands of poor, black slum dwellers were about to be foisted on this community. Thus, many of those most in support of the concept of scatter-site housing turned with a vengeance on the project and the way it was handled.

The city's managing of this affair left something to be desired. The New York *Times* recently revealed that a better proposal was initially accepted and then rejected in part because of "what observers call an intractable housing bureaucracy." But the critics of the project soon were as far removed from reality as its supporters. They created a straw man and whipped it to death. The straw man was the stereotype of a neighborhood about to be overwhelmed by crime, urban decay and declining property values.

As New York Congressman Herman Badillo noted, the facts simply did not support the rhetoric. Thousands of residents of Forest Hills already lived in high-rise apartments a few blocks away. So 840 more units, as proposed in the low-income project, were not likely to alter the neighborhood's character. Moreover, 40 percent of the units were reserved for the elderly, who certainly are not generally responsible for the crime and violence critics were predicting. The remaining units in the project were to be set aside on a preferential basis for residents of Queens, the borough of which Forest Hills is a part. More than 400 such applications were already on file, negating the picture of an onrush of outsiders threatening to destroy the community.

Projections were made that 65 percent of the occupants would be white, so that only 275 apartments would be occupied by blacks and Puerto Ricans. Two hundred minority-group families in a similar project had successfully been integrated into a community close to Forest Hills, demonstrating that the neighborhood would not necessarily become all black.

The fashionable response to these problems is to invoke the new magic words. They generate a mysterious aura for us, as in "land-use planning," "national growth policy" and "urban strategies." All of them—once they are defined—are laudable theories or goals. And all of them soon become the preserve of an in-group of experts who spend long hours formulating huge, largely abstract plans for the America of the twenty-first century. We have not gotten very far with these projections because the man on the street does not have any idea what we are talking about.

There are those who will say that the opinions and understanding of the man in the street are not essential, that if policy planners must wait for the man in the street to be with them no progress will ever be achieved. I don't buy that. Had New York City officials made more of an effort to inform the average, ordinary citizens of Forest Hills what that low-income housing project consisted of they might have met less of the resistance they ultimately faced. I have been in politics long enough to know that no idea will become a successful strategy until people can understand it. Until we recognize that the feelings of the people we are asking to change are as important as the feelings of the people we are trying to help, we will meet stubborn opposition at every turn, even from places assumed to be pockets of support.

There is a related point. It is too easy to formulate plans that look great on paper and have little to do with the real world. An example can be found in the

Pruitt-Igoe Housing project in St. Louis. Pruitt-Igoe was a fifty-seven-acre area cleared away in the early 1950s for construction of forty-three eleven-story apartment buildings for the poor, many of whom had been made homeless by other federal programs such as urban renewal. Total cost of Pruitt-Igoe was about $36 million. In its conception, Pruitt-Igoe was considered the ultimate in public housing. *Architectural Forum* acclaimed it for setting new standards of design. It received an architectural reward for excellence from the American Institute of Architects, the top professional society.

Today, sixteen years after its completion, Pruitt-Igoe is a disaster. The city of St. Louis holds it in very low esteem. In fact, city officials have just received permission to begin to tear part of the project down and start all over again. Over three-fourths of its 2,800 apartments have been abandoned. Rows of Pruitt-Igoe's deserted, windowless buildings loom against the St. Louis skyline like a modern ghost town. Those hallways still used by tenants have become a haven for junkies and muggers. One sociologist calls Pruitt-Igoe "a household term for the worst in ghetto living." The project is a "vertical slum," offering to its tenants conditions and a way of life not much removed from the squalor they are trying to escape.

One of the architects who worked on the design of the project, George Kassabaum, acknowledged that he and others failed because "you had middle-class whites designing something for an entirely different group." Such features as spacious breezeways on every floor, which looked good on the planning board, proved well-suited for "rapists and vandals," Mr. Kassabaum said. He noted that planners misjudged what would be the typical family size by building far too many one- and two-bedroom apartments and not enough four- and five-bedroom dwellings. Then, in a candid and revealing observation, Mr. Kassabaum pointed out, "Our client was the federal government—not the people who were going to live there."

Such a massive project should never have been built in the first place. Pruitt-Igoe is a textbook example of the textbook mentality of too many of our housing policy theorists. They have forgotten that people—not theories—live in homes and apartments and that families rarely consult sociology textbooks before they decide to rent or buy a new dwelling. Too many federal housing ventures are predicated on a vision of the world as someone thinks it should be, instead of a realistic assessment of the world as it is.

New towns, for instance, are an exciting concept for many planners because they are enthusiastic about the idea of starting out from scratch and not having to contend with the mistakes of the past or the pressure groups of the present. There is much to be said in favor of new towns and what they teach us. Reston, Virginia, and Columbia, Maryland, are interesting communities of 15,000 to 18,000 people. One day they will be even larger, housing anywhere from 80,000 to 110,000. They took years of effort, planning and investment to build even to their present size. In the next twenty-five years, we might build ten or even a hundred more new towns like them, housing anywhere from 500,000 to 5 million people. But at the same time, 90 million new home-owners and apartment dwellers will be living some-where in this country. Their communities will be built, shaped and influenced not so much by theorists as by the forces of the market place, politics, highway development, narrow-mindedness and idealism and all the other forces that pull and push against each other and decide for us what our cities, suburbs and countryside will be like.

I am not saying that moving to Reston or Columbia is wrong. I am for new towns, and have intro-duced legislation to provide more federal support for them. But I also recognize that new towns like Res-ton and Columbia will constitute a very small per-centage of communities where our people will be living for the next quarter-century. New towns are not the future, unfortunate as that may be.

It is time we began to spend a little less effort on abstract theories of planning and new towns that we have to generate support for from the ground up. We should spend more time taking a hard look at the forces already at work in our society. If we could harness the momentum and energy that now exist in our society and channel it in directions we feel are useful, we would do more for "urban growth policies" than has ever been done before.

I propose, therefore, that we implement a policy of national growth based on the world as it is and the forces that exist rather than the world as we wish it were and forces that we would like to conjure up if we could. Too often we have tried to tell people where to go—or developed policies based on where we thought they should go—without finding out where they wanted to go and, in fact, in many cases were going anyway. We are all arguing about saving the cities in the face of a clear population explosion in the suburbs. We bewail the evils of a federal highway system while concrete continues to pour and motorists adjust their lives accordingly. We keep winning battles and losing wars as in school integration in the South where we have succeeded in integrating the schools only to find that entire cities are becoming segregated.

Our most successful national growth policies in the past have been those founded on directing the natural inclination of people in directions we thought socially desirable. During America's first century, as population expanded on the East Coast and people sought new opportunities, the federal government successfully dispersed the population westward by subsidizing turnpikes, railroads and river navigation and by opening public lands for settlement. The National Road, Erie Canal, Transcontinental Railroad, Oklahoma land rush and the Homestead Act did not just happen. They were all part of a government policy to move people westward, away from the East Coast. Later, less direct programs, such as reclamation and rural electrification, served similar purposes.

All of our growth policies, unfortunately, have not been planned—or at least openly expressed. Much of the present development of white suburbs and urban sprawl has been sponsored and subsidized by the federal government and its programs. Although imperceptibly, government policies to increase mobility have changed to policies to restrict it. The interstate highway system has combined with federal housing subsidy programs actually to encourage whites to flee the central cities. We laid the first bricks in the exclusionary suburban wall with our own hands.

The irony is that many of those suburbanites now outspoken in their opposition to federally subsidized housing in their communities are living in houses built—and segregated—by the federal government. The FHA home mortgage program has allowed millions of Americans to own their own homes with government assistance. We have all known that and supported it. What many of us did not realize until recently was that we were also supporting blatant racial discrimination. The FHA underwriting manual stated in 1938 and again in 1949 that: "Usually the protection from adverse influences afforded by these means includes prevention of the infiltration of business and industrial uses, lower class occupancies, and inharmonious racial groups."

Of course, as has been often noted, while the FHA was segregating housing in the late 1940s and throughout the 1950s, two out of three homes built in this country were financed without federal assistance. Nonetheless, as George Romney, Secretary of the Department of Housing and Urban Development, admitted in August 1970, the federal government's leadership role during this entire period was one which legitimized racial covenants and lily white suburbs.

Secretary Romney claimed that FHA's policies

"have changed, of course." And yet, almost one year later, the United States Commission on Civil Rights found that FHA was using the newest low- and moderate-income housing programs (the so-called 235 and 236 programs established in 1968) to perpetuate segregation. The programs were building new homes for whites in the suburbs and providing older and sometimes dilapidated homes for blacks in the central cities.

The FHA has had help, of course. Assistance has come from our urban renewal programs, cynically known by poor families in central cities as "urban removal" or "black removal" depending upon your perspective. Urban renewal has destroyed 55,000 units of housing in the last twenty years. In addition, urban renewal together with highway construction and other federal programs destroyed more housing units in the past decade than all the dwellings we built with federal housing subsidies since 1960.

Substantial credit for the suburbs also has to go to the federal highway program. The interstate highway system was proposed in 1955 by President Eisenhower to provide evacuation routes from cities facing atomic attack and pathways for rescue forces. At least 70 million Americans could be saved from holocaust, the theory went, and Congress therefore authorized the most massive public works program in the history of mankind.

The original theory behind the highway program has now gone the way of backyard bomb shelters. But the concrete ribbons keep expanding. As far as the suburbs are concerned, the evacuation allowed was of a more permanent nature than originally envisioned. Instead of the "Red" menace, the enemy soon was seen as the "black" menace. The highways allowed us to keep our jobs in the central cities but retreat every night to the sanctuary of the suburbs.

The busy commuter racing back and forth to town is now being outnumbered by his neighbor who works as well as lives in the suburbs, reflecting the development of jobs in these areas. Nonresidential building permits reveal that in the last five business-census years about 75 percent of all metropolitan industrial buildings were constructed outside the central cities. The Suburban Action Institute found that the forty largest metropolitan areas gained 5.1 million jobs in manufacturing, wholesale and retail trade and related services in the last five years. The suburbs gained 4,370,000 or 85 percent of these jobs.

The U.S. Census Bureau estimates that the number of men employed in central cities declined by 2 percent from 1960 to 1970. At the same time, male employment outside the central cities increased by

35.4 percent. In St. Louis during this period, jobs in the central city declined by 9 percent while those in the surrounding suburbs rose 144 percent. In Baltimore jobs in the suburbs went up 161 percent but in the city itself new positions increased by only 6 percent. In Washington, D.C., while central-city jobs rose 38 percent, those in the suburbs were up by 352 percent.

The ability to invite new business while assuming few of the burdens of this development contributed to the suburbs' rise to prominence, independence and prosperity. It also directly undercut the central city. About eight times as much money must be spent to provide city services to the poor as to the middle class. Consider any big-city mayor's plight when he witnesses a factory leaving his town and moving to the nearby suburbs. Or a new company from another state may simply locate in the suburb of the city. In any event, the lower-paid employees of the installation remain in the city and commute to their jobs if they can. Others may not be able to commute, and may lose their jobs and be unable to find new ones in the dwindling inner-city job market. The city loses the revenues provided by the factory while still providing city services to the working families. The suburban community enjoys the tax revenues from the new plant—but provides no services to the low- and moderate-income employees.

The problem is more complicated than simply the flight of industry to the suburbs. The evidence suggests that for some suburban job growth the term "flight" is a misnomer. New jobs often result from development of new businesses or expansion of existing plants already in the suburbs. The Department of Labor found, for example, that the expansion of manufacturing employment in the suburbs has been mostly in new types of industry such as electronics, aircraft and aerospace. The Suburban Action study showed that the forty metropolitan areas examined gained 2,080,000 manufacturing jobs, 2,055,000 or 99 percent of which went to the suburbs. This expansion has been followed by retail firms and a variety of service industries. Employment in the central city increasingly is concentrated in finance, insurance, communications and corporate headquarters.

Industrial development in the suburbs has been greatly aided by our newest ingredient in the highway game: the suburban "beltway," as it is called in Washington and Baltimore; or the "loop" in Houston; or the "Perimeter" in Atlanta—or, as one developer calls it, "the ribbon of gold." Again, we have a federal program with its avowed purpose overshadowed by its actual impact. Beltways were designed partly to keep the highway program expanding but also to provide a bypass around cities for long-haul travelers. This would also, the theory went, relieve congestion downtown. In addition, the beltway would link suburban cities and major highway arteries.

What actually happened was that the beltways generated an enormous building boom in their immediate vicinity that accelerated the flight of the white and the affluent from the central city. Instead of relieving congestion, the beltways increased it. Rush hour on the beltway now runs from early morning to late at night. In 1968 suburb-to-suburb commuting in Washington made up 41 percent of all trips on the beltway compared to 31 percent at the start of the decade. As many residents of Westchester County in New York now commute within the county as commute in to New York City. Pasadena, Texas, near the Houston loop plans to double and redouble its growth. As Pasadena Mayor Clyde Doyal says, "We have no bus station, no railroad, no airport; what we've got is a freeway." Anyone who doubts this phenomenon merely has to journey along a beltway and note the tremendous development at interchanges with other major highways.

The federal government also has assisted the deterioration of the central cities by beginning to locate more and more of its facilities in suburban areas.

The Post Office plans to decentralize much of its work to suburban locations. The Social Security Administration and the Geological Survey in the nation's capital are racing to new locations thirty miles from downtown Washington. The impact of such moves on the surrounding communities is significant. Location of a major installation in a community often sets in motion dramatic physical, economic and demographic changes. New services start up to serve the people coming in and often provide an impetus for other private or governmental development.

The Civil Rights Commission has documented the effect location of NASA's Manned Spacecraft Center has had on the area of Clear Lake, Texas, about twenty-five miles southeast of Houston. Since 1960, the population surrounding the center has increased 600 percent from 6,500 to 40,000. Total area bank deposits rose from $4.8 million in one bank in 1961 to $30.9 million in five banks in 1966. NASA has estimated that for every 100 jobs at the center an additional 65 jobs have been generated on the outside. The mere presence of the center has caused an influx of over 125 aerospace firms alone.

And, if all this were not enough, our federal farm programs, by ignoring the problems of rural poverty, have helped encourage millions of the rural poor to journey to our central cities. A century ago almost

75

half of all Americans worked the land. Fifty years ago, the number was one in four. Today only one in twenty remains on the farm. Many others still live in the rural areas—often in unimaginable poverty—but most have now traded rural poverty for urban poverty. Since the suburbs are basically home only for those of substance, the central cities have had to absorb yet another influx of immigrants, this time, Americans.

Of course, we should not forget the greatest growth policy of them all—large-lot zoning. While not federally initiated, large-lot zoning has been federally acknowledged and tolerated if not actually encouraged. Land is available in the suburbs upon which to build low- and moderate-income housing. But this kind of dwelling has been kept out of many suburban areas because of large-lot zoning, which is fine for the family that can buy a $70,000 home— they expect a big lot—but excludes the potential home buyer whose means are more modest. Some suburban areas provide for no low-density multifamily zoning, again an effective bar to families of little means.

In general, the only growth policy in the suburbs is a negative one, making it all but impossible for low-income families to live near their suburban jobs. In Mahwah, New Jersey, for example, only eighty-eight

—or 2 percent—of the 4,200 workers at a Ford Motor Company plant live in Mahwah itself. Low- and moderate-income housing is not available in Mahwah, forcing many workers to live in New York City or Newark, both about twenty-five miles away.

So there it is—our national growth policy. It is hard to imagine one more designed to aggravate and inflame the tensions that inevitably exist in a society as diverse as ours. The anthropologists of the next century may shake their heads when trying to make sense of a society that put new, low-income jobs in the suburbs, far beyond the low-income workers mired in the central city, and at the same time kept many white-collar jobs concentrated in the central cities, where office space continues to be built miles away from most of the suburbanites holding those jobs. The population of Newark, New Jersey, for example, is 400,000. This doubles every day as a result of the influx of workers from the suburbs, a process repeated in city after city across this country. The "commuter's crawl" every morning is our own just reward.

We are, in more ways than one, reaping what we have sown. Housing shortages, racial segregation and ethnic isolation, class conflicts, urban crime, frightened suburbanites, endless highways leading farther and farther from cities we say we are trying to save—

77

all this and more are a harvest of mixed-up, confused, and conflicting land-use policies, policies that must be junked or reformed or replaced.

IV

Housing—Some Solutions

WE HAVE SEEN how federal policies work at cross purposes with each other, how taxpayers' dollars are spent, on the one hand, to save the cities while, on the other, taxpayers' dollars are invested in highway development which only drains more life from the cities. Government programs have worked to solidify the virtually all-white complexion of most suburban communities while other federal efforts ostensibly are designed to promote fair and color-blind housing practices. We want to encourage rural families to stay in the countryside. Yet we do little to make their lives on the farm more comfortable and inviting and seem to go out of our way to prompt them to feel their opportunities are in the cities.

The one characteristic federal land-use and community-development policies share in common is that they seem to have been formulated and implemented alone and apart from each other, as if no one of them was related to or had an impact on any other. In short, our land-use and community-development programs are a hodgepodge desperately in need of review, and reform.

We must begin, as I have already noted, by working with the forces already at play in society. Only then can we succeed. Good arguments can be made, for example, that more if not most of the money we now spend on highways should be spent on new and improved systems of mass transportation. I will continue to believe that. But at the same time, we can be sure that the political reality is such that highways and beltways will continue to be built. We can stand around wringing our hands about this and let history repeat itself in the next series of outer beltways that will be built, or we can begin to formulate plans to channel the forces behind highway development in such a way as to make them a force for improvement in the community. Why make it an either-or equation? Trying to improve the way we build highways is not at all inconsistent with expanding our system of mass transportation.

Similarly, we can develop programs to help the central cities, but at the same time millions of new jobs will be opening in the suburbs and beyond. Much of this growth is natural since many modern industries need massive amounts of land for production facilities that once covered several stories downtown and now rise only one story but cover an area equal to hundreds of city blocks. Again, the question is not whether industry will continue to locate in the open spaces—it will. The question is whether we're going to stand idly by bemoaning our fate and accomplishing nothing or whether we're going to work to harness that natural movement for the benefit of society.

In short, a path of development exists in various forms in areas across this country. We should move ourselves into that path and work to direct it toward accepted national goals. It may well be that if we can successfully develop the new growth centers of this country so that they are open to all, even those from the central cities, and if we can make rural life more viable for those who would like to remain there, we will find that much of the pressure on the central cities has been alleviated.

Our ultimate goal ought to be a national policy designed to give all Americans the right to move and live where they please to the maximum extent possible. The poor white Appalachian farmer who is forced off the land and into the Chicago slums because there are no rural jobs has no real freedom of mobility. The black family in the inner city which cannot find decent housing in the suburbs has no freedom of movement. A combination of deliberate and inadvertent governmental policies has effectively trapped these Americans into a particular mode of living. They can do little to correct it without some help.

The first force we must deal with is the continuing development of the suburbs. Industry's need for land provides a continual pressure for expansion into suburban areas. In addition, the housing industry is finding that land costs and availability are dictating moves into the suburbs. Vacant land is plentiful within twenty to thirty miles of every major central city in this country. At the same time costs are increasing in the central city. In New York City, it costs more than $30,000 per unit to build public housing that could be built in the form of row houses and garden apartments for less than $20,000 a unit in the suburbs.

Land prices are so high in the central cities it is economically unreasonable to build anything less than the most expensive dwellings. For example, the average cost of land purchased under the urban renewal programs ranged from $76,000 per acre in Atlanta to $695,000 in New York City. At the same time, one acre on the suburban fringe costs only $3,000. Furthermore, less than 2 percent of the vacant central city land is zoned for residential use. The situation is such that Mayor Alfonso J. Cervantes, of St. Louis, told Jack Rosenthal, of the New York *Times:* "Do you know how many houses were started in the city last year [1969]? Fourteen." Mr. Rosenthal asked, did he mean fourteen hundred? "No," Mayor Cervantes answered, "fourteen."

At present, however, housing in the suburbs is beyond the reach of most Americans. The median sales price for an existing single family home is now more than $25,000. The average cost of a new home in Montgomery County, Maryland, a Washington suburb, is more than $40,000 and virtually no homes in the $15,000 to $25,000 range are being built. Almost two-thirds of the housing on the market throughout the nation is above the level that a family with an $8,000 income can afford. This means that the people who need the jobs opening up in the suburbs are precluded from living there. They are trapped in the central city. The result is a scarcity of needed employment for the poor and in some cases an actual shortage of low- and moderate-income employees for suburban concerns. Numerous suburbs are now discovering that they have priced their teachers, firemen, police and other municipal employees out of their communities.

The situation is going to get worse before it gets better. For example, the twenty local governments in a 400-square-mile area around Princeton, New Jersey, have zoned enough underdeveloped land for industry and research firms to support 1.2 million new jobs. The same towns, however, have zoned the remaining land to house only 144,000 workers—about one-tenth of the potential work force. Low-income workers will be forced to commute from Camden or Newark or even New York, cities which will end up assuming the costs the suburbs avoid.

Improved public transportation programs are often offered as a solution. There is no doubt that existing transit systems are inadequate and only aggravate matters. They are designed to serve suburbanites, not urban dwellers. Transportation systems are organized to bring suburbanites into the city in the morning and out again at night. The urban highway networks serve middle- and upper-income workers and professionals who can afford to live in the suburbs and own a car. But they are useless to low-income workers who cannot live in suburbia or own an automobile.

The majority of low-income employees, who rely on public transit to reach their jobs, find even getting to inner-city jobs is a difficult task. To get out to the new jobs in the suburbs is next to impossible because of the time and cost involved. Residents of outlying Maryland suburbs reach the Washington central city each morning and leave each night on express buses which take an average of thirty-six minutes each way. For a person going in the opposite direction at the same time to a job in the suburbs, the trip averages fifty-four minutes each way and usually involves two transfers.

Improving mass transportation out to the suburbs would help, therefore, but will not solve the problem. Many "reverse commuter" experiments have been tried and most have proven uneconomical. Suburban job locations, like the suburbs themselves, are too dispersed to warrant, in economic terms, operating separate transportation systems.

More must be done. But the first response from many people—particularly the socially concerned— is that we should do nothing to assist the development of the suburbs. My answer to that is that they are going to "develop" one way or the other, whether we like it or not. The only question is, will we be able to influence that development?

Much of the objection to the suburbs reflects a prejudice among the intelligentsia against these communities. Many sociologists, commentators and social critics give low marks to suburban culture. Urban means urbane, they say; urban civilization represents sophistication, art, tolerance and intellectual pursuits while suburbia is sterile and cut off from the flesh and blood of life.

Whether or not the suburban culture is a good one, preferable to urban civilization, depends on the viewer. The very term "suburbs" means many things. The word covers a wide variety of communities, from those resembling the usual suburban image of split-level houses and wide lawns to others that have nothing to do with this picture. In suburbia, we also find farm communities, city-size factory towns, dense clusters of medium- to high-rise apartments and office buildings. Baltimore County, for example, is an unusually diverse suburb. Within its boundaries are one of the world's largest steel plants and nearly 2,000 farms, urban centers, rural villages, massive apartment developments and rolling estates.

If we try to convince most Americans to live somewhere because of the sophistication, art, tolerance and intellectual environment, we will win few converts. Most Americans are more inclined to settle someplace where land is cheap, streets are wide, parking is available, crime is not prevalent, local taxes are low, public services are adequate and housing is well within their income.

Too often we have forgotten that the suburbs represent new opportunity for families trying to move up the socioeconomic ladder. Many Americans, particularly those whose experience in America is only one or two generations old, see a home in the suburbs as a step upward, an indication that they are bettering themselves. Many ordinary people find in the suburbs a realization of the promise of America. "The suburban house," says Edgardo Contini, a noted urbanist, "is the realization of every immigrant's dream—the vassal's dream of his own castle. Europeans who come here are delighted by our suburbs, even by the worst sprawl. Not to live in an apartment! It is a universal aspiration to own your own home." We should make the fulfillment of that aspiration possible for more Americans.

As we try to influence the development of the suburbs, we should recognize that we face two different problems. One is the question of how we are going to work with established suburbs, generally close to the central city. The other is how we are going to respond to the areas in the next ring that are just beginning to grow and where most of the growth in the next thirty years will occur.

Beginning with the inner suburbs, our policy should be that a community may choose to continue just as it is, so long as it does not receive or benefit from federal assistance. In many cases there is not much more room in these areas in any event for new housing or industry. However, if a community wants to attract a new industry or federal facility, or if it chooses to participate in a federal program like urban renewal or revenue sharing, then that community should have an obligation to assume a reasonable share of the responsibilities for housing the workers of the plant or federal facility and the low- and moderate-income people of the metropolitan area.

As a first step, I introduced legislation last year that would empower the federal government to have its own suburban facilities and the suburban facilities of its contractors located and expanded only in areas where communities are willing to provide low- and moderate-income housing for the workers of those facilities.

This legislation—the Government Facilities Location Act—recognizes the difficult financial plight in which many suburbs now find themselves. Much of the opposition to the provision of low- and moderate-income housing in these areas stems from fears that taxes will have to be raised to maintain existing levels of municipal services, particularly education. This fear comes not only from affluent members of the community but also from many middle-income families already there who fear the impact on school budgets of having to educate more children, regardless of their color.

Since as much as 50 to 60 percent of many suburban budgets is devoted to education, my bill provides assistance for education to any suburb that makes available the needed housing. Some have argued that no assistance should be provided to such suburbs. The mere fact that the facility locates in their community should be sufficient incentive. In many cases, that may be true. But I am equally concerned about the numerous suburbs that would be willing to cooperate if they were assured that the level of their educational activities would not suffer or be burdened by new arrivals.

An analysis of the Massachusetts antisnob zoning law has shown that a major reason for its ineffectiveness is that it ignores the economic and tax consequences imposed on suburbs that admit low- and moderate-income people. In particular, the failure to adjust school aid formulas for suburbs has been highlighted as a major area of concern.

The immediate picture conjured up in the minds of most suburbanites at this point is the specter of their community turning into an all-black slum or massive public-housing projects thrust artificially and arbitrarily into their neighborhoods. The picture is false. The workers in the plants and facilities obviously are not welfare recipients. They have jobs, in fact, the very jobs the suburbs are trying to attract. It is not asking too much for a community that obtains the benefit of a new industry to shoulder the responsibilities that go with it and provide housing opportunities for these workers and their families.

Almost two years ago, an uproar was raised when the Department of Housing and Urban Development considered requiring the city of Warren, Michigan, to provide units of low- and moderate-income housing in conjunction with a federally financed urban renewal program. Ultimately, HUD backed down. What many people did not realize, however, was that about 30 percent of Warren's work force—mainly in automobile-related plants—was black, and virtually none of those workers lived in Warren. One survey revealed twenty-eight black families among Warren's 180,000 people. That is an intolerable situation that strongly suggests blacks were not allowed to live in Warren.

If the people of Warren wanted to maintain their community as it was, they could have gone ahead, hoping they violated no laws. But they were asking the federal government for $2.8 million for an urban renewal program to improve their city. That is a laudable goal. But why should the federal government subsidize exclusionary housing practices that prevent thousands of workers from living near their jobs?

On the other hand, it is too easy to simply wipe off the people of Warren as bigots who deserve none of our time or concern. Warren is basically a blue-collar, working-class community, and those people have more than their share of problems, as I will discuss in the next chapter. By their housing patterns and attitudes—and their desire for urban renewal funds—the citizens of Warren were only doing what came naturally in the contradictory environment of federal programs.

The opposition of suburban communities such as Warren to federal housing programs is not totally irrational. These programs have often been abominations—both for the community in which they have been located and for the people who live in them. The Pruitt-Igoe housing project in St. Louis is only an example of this phenomenon. Because the government would not attempt to open up the suburbs, it was forced to sponsor or support projects similar to Pruitt-Igoe in every major city. They were not all as large as Pruitt-Igoe—nor as unsuccessful—but each was an unnecessary concentration of a racial and economic group. Given the ingredients and the environment, the problems which arose could have been predicted, but weren't.

Projects such as Pruitt-Igoe are a perversion of the concept of publicly assisted housing. Nineteenth-century English policy was founded wisely on the principle that the cheapest and most wholesome form of housing for working-class families was the attached house or row house with a common, shared open-space area. Conversely, we have always seen low- and moderate-income housing in terms of massive "projects" often built on the most expensive land. These projects have only concentrated problems of crime and violence, thereby adding to the convenient stereotype that every federally assisted housing project is filthy and crime-ridden and destined to become a blot on any neighborhood unfortunate enough to find such a building in its area.

There are alternatives to this approach. I toured housing projects in Scandinavia two years ago. When inspecting one area in Sweden, I asked the guide if we were in a low-income neighborhood. He looked puzzled for a moment and then explained that there was no low-income housing or moderate-income housing in Sweden—there was just housing. Assistance varied according to income. But everyone lived in a standard, basically sound unit.

We also need to broaden our perspective when we talk about where to build federally supported housing. As with the problems of school integration, the common assumption that the first blacks or poor people in a neighborhood are only the first of hordes does not hold up if we view matters on a metropolitan-wide scale. There just are not enough poor or black people to dominate any city in an area, if everyone participates equally. The 1970 census revealed that over 90 percent of the major metropolitan areas in this country had a black population of less than 25 percent.

An exciting program is being tried now in the Dayton metropolitan area under the guidance of the Miami Valley Regional Planning Commission. Like many new programs, it has had its ups and downs and also runs the danger of being overinterpreted or overgeneralized as its success becomes more apparent. Nonetheless, it has been successful in one of the most difficult problem areas we face.

Basically, the Dayton plan is an agreement by all the suburbs of Dayton—predominantly white, but ranging from very wealthy to working-class—to provide a certain percentage of the low-income housing that is needed in the metropolitan area. Five counties surrounding Dayton are participating. Dayton's population is 244,000, about 30 percent of which is black. The five-county population is nearly 900,000. The critical point is that blacks make up only 11 percent of the metropolitan area's population, a phenomenon repeated in most metropolitan areas in this country. In Dayton, we see an example of how, through a program of mutual cooperation, one metropolitan area plans to provide 14,000 additional low- and moderate-income housing units over the next four years without forcing any community to become the new "slum."

The Dayton agreement did not just happen magically overnight, of course. A careful study was made of the housing needs of the area and units were assigned to areas on the basis of school capacity, population and the number of low-income units already in the community. An extensive educational campaign by community leaders, the media and members of the Dayton "establishment" followed.

Dale Bertsch, the executive director of the program, told me recently at a Senate hearing that the program could never have worked without widespread community support. Of particular importance, he said, was the thorough effort to explain carefully to every community involved that no neighborhood would be overrun with the poor and that public housing was no longer going to be built in the huge projects so many objected to. A twenty-six-unit public housing development in a white, blue-collar neighborhood, for example, was originally vigorously opposed by residents. The completed brick townhouses are now the most attractive in the area and black and white families are living there without difficulty.

The Dayton plan has years to go. But it stands as an illustration of what can be accomplished if we begin to look at the problems of housing low- and moderate-income families on a metropolitan-wide basis, rather than forcing one or two cities to bear the burden alone and then shaking our heads knowingly when the inevitable neighborhood deterioration results.

We will still have to recognize that some communities are going to refuse to change their ways. We should work to overcome their fears and objections. Programs like the one in Dayton take us a long way in that direction. But ultimately we may have to leave the few recalcitrants alone, as long as they don't ask us to subsidize the standard of living to which they have become accustomed.

I know there will be objections to this position. It is always a good way to show you are committed to the "cause" to advocate that everyone be dragged and forced into compliance with our views. But I don't think that will work here. The number of communities that will not voluntarily cooperate with their neighbors and that need no assistance from the federal government, especially if we adopt a revenue-sharing program, will be few. Perhaps that small "escape" valve—or even medium-sized one—is important if we are not to have this question deteriorate to the level of vague, meaningless rhetoric that now surrounds debates on issues such as "busing" and "public housing."

In addition we need to focus more of our energies on the newly expanding areas of this country where the federal government is deeply involved. Ultimately, the 90 million people we expect to add in the next thirty years are not going to be added in the central cities, or in the well-established suburbs where the most vocal objections to low- and moderate-income housing are heard. The population expansion is going on beyond those areas in the second ring of suburbs, communities like Rockville and Gaithersburg outside of Washington, the Nassau County cities outside New York City and Pasadena City outside Houston.

It is in communities like these that we should make our stand, for otherwise the scenario for the future is clear. Without federal planning, we will simply proceed to complete the ring of beltways around our major cities and begin construction of another series of outer loops or beltways, all of which will generate an enormous growth in population and expansion of industry, as has occurred around the beltways already completed.

New suburbs will spring up haphazardly, industry will continue to move farther away from both the central city and, inevitably, the inner suburbs. The white, more affluent residents of these areas will follow along. The inner suburbs will age and decline. Their housing stock is often poorly constructed frame dwellings that already are beginning to deteriorate. New migration will begin. We will finally "integrate" these older suburbs. For a few years everyone will cheer. Then we will notice that the inner suburbs are getting poorer and poorer, and blacker and blacker. In short, they will go the way of the central cities.

This may take some time. How long is not certain. But it is certain that it will happen. The cycle has already begun. The 1970 census showed that, while the percentage of blacks in the suburbs remained the same, about 4.5 percent, the number increased with the increase in population. Thus, 762,000 more blacks lived in the suburbs in 1970 than in 1960. But 12.5 million whites also moved to the suburbs during that time. More importantly, most of the blacks moving to the suburbs were simply moving from one ghetto to another.

In the Washington area, for example, three-fourths of the increase in black school enrollment in the suburbs occurred in one county, Prince George's. In the Dayton metropolitan area discussed earlier, the mayor of Trotwood, a Dayton suburb, made it clear that his constituents desperately supported the joint plan. "If we don't have this plan, this umbrella," he said, "we'll be inundated long before other communities have any [blacks]."

It is time to head off the fleeing suburbanites at the pass. Their new communities are going to develop with federal assistance and we should do everything we can to avoid, through direct or inadvertent federal actions, encouraging more of the same—that is, racial and economic segregation. It should be easier to do in the communities of the future.

Integrating an existing community threatens the expectations of those who bought homes in that community because they liked it for exactly what it was. Why not change those expectations in the new growth areas before people move in? Why not state as firm policy that everyone who moves into one of these areas is going to find a reasonable amount of economic and racial integration? If he doesn't like it, let him go somewhere else—so long as it's not an area getting federal assistance. Ninety million people are going to be living in new communities by the year 2000. I would hope that at least those communities could be living demonstrations of the American ideal of equal rights for all that we have claimed for all these years.

The Department of Transportation has begun a small program designed to demonstrate "that areas with a potential for economic growth can be aided by highways." We don't have to convince anyone of that. What we need to do is demonstrate that well-planned highways can lead to urban, suburban and rural living that is consistent with and encourages the development of a unified society.

Highway engineers should be working hand in hand with planners at the Department of Housing and Urban Development and other federal agencies involved in city programs. The federal government itself should start buying some of the valuable land near beltways and selling the land to developers who will contract to build mixed-income developments with a specified proportion of low- and moderate-income families. We should, in short, convert our federal highway program into a positive force for community development in the metropolitan areas of this country.

The new communities we foster should be large

enough to provide diversity of services and social and cultural opportunities, but small enough to be governable and offer all their citizens the chance to involve themselves in civic affairs. In this age of bigness, one of the great challenges we face is to restore to our people's lives a sense of community. Somehow we have to learn to make our governmental jurisdictions small and responsive enough so that people can relate to them and their leaders.

In his unsuccessful effort to be elected mayor of New York, Norman Mailer proposed several valid ideas, one of which I have long supported. It was to dismantle New York City's government and divide it up into smaller governing units. That way the citizenry could enjoy the sense of belonging to something personal and humane. Public services, then, administered by managers and civil servants who were themselves closer to the people, would improve. Reporting from England, New York *Times* correspondent Anthony Lewis commented along similar lines. He pointed out that London, in spite of its mammoth size, has achieved a measure of that sense of belonging. London, he reports, is a big city split into boroughs that have real functions and into neighborhoods that keep their own character. "To a happy extent," Mr. Lewis observes, "London remains a collection of villages within a cosmopolitan whole."

The communities I envision should not be dominated by any single industry or institution—we should avoid "company towns," no matter what their vintage—but should contain within them at least one major commercial or public institution and satellite enterprises with a vocational school, community college or university nearby. Many states could learn from the California example where towns with populations as small as 10,000 or 15,000 have community colleges which serve not only as vocational and adult education schools but also as steppingstones for young men and women wishing to qualify for the state college or university system. In short, the communities of the future should be governable, reasonably self-sufficient and organized not so much on the hunger for growth but on the potential for individual fulfillment.

But even doing all this will not solve our problems entirely, for those leaving our central cities are only half the picture. Millions of Americans are moving into the cities. Many of them are the rural poor, and they are coming to the cities because urban life, from a distance, seems more comfortable to them. The rural poor are completing the great migration from the farm to the cities. In 1790, 95 percent of our people lived in rural areas. By 1900 this percentage had dropped to 60 percent. In the last ten years, the percentage dropped further, from 30 percent to less than 25 percent.

The city seems to the rural poor as a land of opportunity. For some, the cities fulfill that promise. But most would have been as well off, if not better off, had they stayed down on the farm. Here is another example of federal policy that has worked at cross purposes with itself and other federal policies and frequently has made conditions worse.

For years, our farm policy has basically been a question of assuring price stability for farm products, the assumption being that this would help everyone living in rural areas. For at least fifteen years, we have known that that assumption was only a charade, that price supports for products were only helpful if there were products to sell. Millions of small farmers across the country did not have that good fortune. And so they got poorer and poorer. Ultimately, they sank into poverty in the rural areas or moved to the cities, where a better fortune generally proved just as cruelly evasive.

Throughout the process, we ignored the human misery involved in this situation. Our almost complete attention has been directed at the urban manifestations of a problem which actually spreads across regional lines. No one has organized to represent rural and small town people the way lobbies have sprung up around urban interests with urban coalitions, institutes and leagues. There is no widely known Rural Coalition, or Rural Institute or Rural League.

Even our commissions become famous only if they are urban-oriented. Many know about the Douglas Commission's study on urban problems and the Kaiser Committee's report on urban housing. The Kerner Commission's report on the cities of this country became a best seller. But few even knew there was a President's Commission on Rural Poverty whose chairman's name never became a shorthand reference for the study. And yet, a 1968 Gallup Poll revealed that 56 percent of those questioned would choose a rural life if they were free to choose. Only 18 percent would choose a city and 25 percent the suburbs. For many, of course, the wish never becomes a reality, because rural areas are always pictured as being somewhere out in the boondocks. But as James Sundquist has noted, if we draw a twenty-five-mile circle around small cities with a proven economic potential demonstrated by their recent growth, we include within those circles most of the country's rural population east of the high plains. A series of fifty-mile circles blankets virtually the entire country.

The rural areas of this country are directly related

to our future growth, even if no further migration occurs to our major central cities. We should develop this relationship as a matter of federal policy. We should do this even without such a relationship to our cities, for the poverty in our rural areas is as intense as anywhere. The truth is that bad housing is more common—both in amount and degree—outside the metropolitan areas. A 1968 survey revealed that 4.7 million housing units were substandard in America. Of these, 3.1 million or 67 percent were outside of metropolitan areas. Put another way, 14 percent of all nonmetropolitan households lived in substandard housing, compared with 4 percent of all metropolitan households.

I discovered recently that a powerful potential coalition exists in the Congress for a joint attack on rural and urban poverty. During the 1971 debate on the President's tax program, Senator James G. Pearson of Kansas offered an amendment designed to attract industry to rural areas. His proposal would have increased the investment tax credit from 7 percent to 10 percent for firms that established job-creating enterprises in rural areas. I thought this was a good idea, and argued that the concept should also apply to job-creating industries that located in central cities with high unemployment.

To my surprise, this joint approach met with enthusiastic support from senators of both parties from across the country. My amendment to Senator Pearson's amendment passed, 56 to 24, and both amendments together then passed, 60 to 19.

While these amendments were deleted from the bill by the Senate-House conference, the lesson was clear: if we are willing to recognize the legitimate problems of rural areas and their poverty, many senators from those areas will support efforts to eliminate or relieve urban poverty. If nothing else, simply making rural areas in this country more livable for more people will substantially alleviate the growing pressures on our central cities. And, if we are to build on existing "growth" centers, or develop "new" towns, there's no better place to begin than in the rural areas of this country.

Figures demonstrate that industry is already beginning to move beyond the cities and the suburbs to these smaller towns and rural areas where land is plentiful. We should be as interested in assuring that those areas provide adequate housing, transportation, schools and hospitals for the industry's workers as we are in ensuring these in metropolitan areas.

I was pleased to read a recent speech by Senator Herman Talmadge of Georgia, chairman of the Senate Agriculture Committee, on the subject of community development. Senator Talmadge said: "It has always amazed me that the federal government, with its tremendous power to affect the economies of the nation's towns and cities, has never established any clear policy for giving an area's population density and its economy some consideration in the location of new facilities."

Because of the needs of his state, Senator Talmadge called for new facilities to be placed in rural areas. While no area should receive all government facility expansion, the fact that senators from the highly urbanized Northeast and the more rural-oriented South are thinking along the same lines illustrates that the urban-rural relationship and the powerful effect of what appear to be relatively simple governmental site-location decisions are beginning to be recognized by more and more people. Senator Talmadge himself said, "Unless we can convince our urban friends that it is to their advantage to support programs which improve living conditions in rural America, programs which will finally stop the interminable migration to the cities, we won't be able to do much more than talk about our problems."

If the President and the Congress refuse to begin to move on these problems, we will soon have a repeat performance by the courts of their role in school integration. In fact, in a few instances, the courts have already moved into the void and begun to rule that federal housing policies cannot be used to increase the housing segregation that already exists. State courts have begun to overturn restrictive suburban-zoning ordinances and building codes, while federal courts have begun to limit the construction of low-income housing in the overcrowded central cities.

In four recent decisions, federal courts have: (1) removed barriers to subsidized housing in white areas, (2) ordered officials to begin building half of a city's new subsidized units in white neighborhoods, (3) banned further federally subsidized housing in racially concentrated city neighborhoods, and (4) ordered local officials to draft a plan to disperse subsidized housing throughout an entire metropolitan area.

While the courts should be applauded for entering the vacuum left by legislative and executive inaction, the consequences are not difficult to predict. Unless the Congress and the President respond, the situation will parallel the school desegregation dilemma. If the courts are forced to desegregate neighborhoods as well as schools, the emotion and confusion already existing will multiply. As Richard Babcock, one of the nation's leading authorities on housing and zoning law, points out, "The almost unlimited variations in fact from one zoning case to another make a school desegregation case appear like simple arithmetic." More important, the refusal by some suburban areas to establish reasonable zoning standards may force the courts to eliminate the system altogether. The end result would be rampant confusion over local land-use policies.

The program in Dayton, Ohio, shows what constructive leadership can accomplish in dealing with one of the most sensitive issues this country faces. But it requires elected and appointed officials willing to infuse the debate with courage and common sense. Sufficient quantities of either commodity have not been apparent these past few years. This country's future is being decided every day as families and industries make their individual decisions about where to move and how to live. It is that natural development of momentum in our society that our leaders must learn to harness if we are ever to be successful.

Perhaps we would increase the likelihood of such success if we looked more realistically at the commitment we seek from the people of this country. For years we have all supported the concept of universal brotherhood and our mutual responsibilities for each other. Yet considerable tension still exists between groups. In some areas, strain and the potential for turmoil are growing.

We would, I think, have more success if we asked

people for a little less love of one another and a lot more mutual respect and tolerance. Let us strive for universal "cousinhood" and hope our grandchildren can achieve the "brotherhood." Ours, after all, is not a homogeneous society the way Sweden, for example, is. In a civilization as diverse as ours, composed of more races, colors and creeds than any other in history, social harmony and accord are important goals, but they are not always achievable.

We are dealing with human beings, and human beings, since Adam, have been known to fall, to have prejudices and to dislike others for no necessarily just or logical reasons. I am reminded of an observation made by George Blanda, the perennial superstar professional quarterback. Recalling the rough-and-tumble coal mine country, Youngwood, Pennsylvania, of his youth, Blanda said, "As a training ground for competitiveness, you couldn't beat Youngwood. We had people subdivided into more nationalities, classes, religions and types than any sociologist ever imagined, and every group competed with every other group. Why, there are people in Youngwood right this minute who look down on me because I'm of Slovak descent, and I guess if I was perfectly honest I'd have to admit that there are certain groups that still bug me. That's the way I was brought up."

That's the way many people are brought up, as a

matter of fact. The least we can ask for, though, is that every member of every group have the chance to do what he or she does best, be it throwing and kicking a football or painting murals. While it may be difficult for the rich and the poor, the blacks and the whites, farmers and city dwellers to love one another, it certainly should not be too much to ask that they learn to understand and coexist with one another a little more. We will find, I believe, that if we cannot demolish the walls that separate us, we can build bridges over those walls that will help to restore stability to our society.

V

The Working Class

FROM WOMB TO TOMB, the American working class is in constant economic insecurity. Unemployment, recession, inflation, medical bills, a lack of educational opportunities, poor housing and the fear of a retirement in poverty are major problems that haunt working families wherever they turn. They feel their government has forgotten them, that their leaders are preoccupied with the problems of blacks and other minorities.

Working Americans are the largest single group in the country, comprising 82 million people, yet they

III

have been aptly described as the Forgotten People. One description of them was made by former Undersecretary of Housing and Urban Development and now president of the University of Massachusetts, Robert D. Wood, who said of the typical head of the working-class household:

> He is a white employed male . . . earning between $5,000 and $10,000. He works regularly, steadily, dependably, wearing a blue collar or white collar. Yet the frontiers of his career expectations have been fixed since he reached the age of 35, when he found that he had too many obligations, too much family and too few skills to match opportunities with aspirations. . . . The working American lives in the gray area fringes of a central city or in a close-in or very far-out cheaper suburban subdivision of a large metropolitan area. He is likely to own a home and a car, especially as his income begins to rise. Of those earning between $6,000 and $7,000, 70 percent own their own homes and 94 percent drive their own cars. Ninety-four percent have no education beyond high school and 43 percent have only completed the eighth grade.

One-third of all Americans live in such families and millions more share their problems or their state of mind.

Consider the daily life of an average working man

and his plight becomes even clearer. Let's call him Joe Taylor. He is forty-one years old, married for twenty-one years and the father of three children. His grandfather, a tailor, came from Poland with the name Zbroszczyk. An immigration official could not pronounce it. So from that moment on, the American branch of the Zbroszczyk family was known as Taylor.

Joe works in a factory, belongs to a union and makes $9,600 a year. He dropped out of high school, went to work at the factory where he has worked ever since and married a girl, Mary, he had known since childhood. Their son Michael is twenty, a Vietnam veteran who cannot find work and is living at home. Another son finishes high school this year, is bright, and has been encouraged by his teachers to go on to college. But Joe does not know where the money will come from. Their daughter, Doris, is twelve. She wants to go to college, too, and Joe does not know where the money will come from for her, either.

The Taylors live in a two-story, twenty-five-year-old, four-bedroom, $17,000 home near the downtown section. Their home has one bathroom. Mary has a clothes washer but not a dryer. She would like a rollaway dishwasher. But that is a luxury they cannot afford now. She would also like a garbage disposal installed. Joe would like to buy a color television set.

Their 21-inch black-and-white model is five years old and starting to fade.

The Taylors are always short of money. Joe makes $800 a month. Federal and state income taxes come to $105 a month. Social Security deductions are $30. Health insurance is $23. Union dues are $7. That leaves Joe a monthly take-home paycheck of $635. Grocery bills are about $200 a month. From the remaining $435, mortgage, telephone, electricity and gas bills take $210, life insurance is $12, and car expenses including insurance and payments $75. Their church receives $2 a Sunday or $8 a month. Joe spends $20 out-of-pocket a month, Mary about the same. Clothing, personal care and other family expenses take up as much as $50. They stubbornly save $30 a month whenever possible. Therefore, if they are lucky—if the sink doesn't stop up, if the children don't catch the flu and if everything else works okay —the Taylors end up each month with about $10 to spare.

The Taylors and millions of working families like them live in a permanent and lifelong economic squeeze. They are quite literally broke all the time. Any sudden, serious illness would wipe them out. It is often impossible to send their children to college. Retirement threatens them with virtually guaranteed poverty. They read about themselves being the highest-paid working people in history. They may even take heart momentarily from that kind of easy assurance. But sooner or later they are bound to detect that the affluence they keep hearing about in this so-called affluent society has not trickled down to their level, and possibly never will.

Along with their frequently desperate economic plight, working men and women increasingly sense a prejudice against them in academic, intellectual and liberal political circles. They know that some commentators and social critics blame many of society's ills on them. They also know an anti-working-class bias can be found in many colleges and elsewhere in our society. Former U.S. Representative Allard Lowenstein, of New York, who sparked the student movement to dump President Johnson in 1968, described the anti-lower-middle-class feeling at the colleges this way: "Many of the young people see middle-class people as nothing but a bunch of big-bosomed, beer-drinking, drum-and-bugle-corps types." Eric Hoffer, the longshoreman-philosopher, says the feeling is mutual, asserting: "We are told we have to feel guilty. We've been poor all our lives and now we're being preached to by every son of a bitch who comes along. The ethnics are discovering that you can't trust Mayflower boys."

S. I. Hayakawa, the semantics professor who became president of San Francisco State College, believes the educated classes are dangerously out of touch with working families. "You and I," he told a reporter, "can live in the suburbs and demand integration in the schools downtown. We can make the moral demands and someone else has to live with them. We can say the war in Vietnam is a dirty, immoral act, while our children are in college, exempt from the draft. The working people's children are in Vietnam, and they're praying for victory. They want to believe America is right."

These men and women look back upon the meager beginning of their families in America and they ask: "We did it without federal grants. Why can't blacks? Why should they have all the special treatment?" It is not that they begrudge blacks progress in seeking to redress past wrongs. But ethnics feel the rules should not be changed now, making it easier for blacks where it was difficult for them. Never mind that most white ethnics, no matter how poor when they started out in this country, came here as agents of Western culture and civilization, to a country that needed millions of unskilled workers, and were allowed to take advantage of the opportunities that the nation offered; while blacks came here in chains, found a civilization alien to the one they had left, suffered through an early existence when family life was not only discouraged but often outlawed, and now find an economy incapable of absorbing those with few skills. The reasons why the blacks have lagged behind are not what the working white critics see. They see only their own condition, compare it with that of blacks, and find the black experience wanting.

Paradoxically, once blacks begin to make gains, the white working people fear those gains will be registered at their expense. They observe the blacks calling for solidarity, for unity, for "putting it all together." To a group threatened, black efforts to organize are interpreted as the first step in new assaults on working people's rights, prerogatives and life styles.

In some instances, fear of economic loss is not a figment of the working-class imagination. Many black gains in housing, education and jobs have direct impact on white working families. It is their neighborhoods into which aspiring blacks move, their schools where blacks are integrated and their jobs which blacks actively compete for. The direct relationship between working whites and aspiring blacks has tended to pit these two groups against each other. White workers start thinking more in terms of white solidarity—rather than worker solidarity. "Why not?" they ask. "The soul brothers are thinking in black-versus-white terms. Why shouldn't we?"

A union member refused to apologize for the closedness of his craft. "Some men leave their sons money," he said, "some large investments, some business connections and some a profession. I have only one worthwhile thing to give: my trade. I hope to follow a centuries-old tradition and sponsor my sons for an apprenticeship. For this simple father's wish it is said that I discriminate against Negroes. Don't all of us discriminate? Which of us . . . will not choose a son over all others?"

Liberals safely ensconced in the professions, business and universities can articulate the bromide that the victory of one man need not be the defeat of another, that rising black membership in unions does not necessarily mean fewer jobs for whites. We can keep making these same assurances to white workers. But white workers, as well as black, know that in an economy with a limited number of jobs, when the black man lands one, it is a job that could have been filled by a white. The equation is simple and does not require a college education. There are x number of jobs. The jobs are all held by white workers. A black wins a job. The number of jobs is now x minus one.

Thus, the liberals and intellectuals seem to be siding with the blacks as far as the working class is concerned. Workers begin to feel it is them against the world—against the blacks, against the liberals, against the Democratic party they help support and elect—all of whom seem bent on reshaping American life at the expense of working people. It isn't fair, they say. Rhetoric escalates. Extreme talk becomes reputable. Polarization sets in. Once in motion, it is difficult to control.

It is at this point that the workers notice there are few people to articulate their thoughts for them. They look around and see that black people are organized and have spokesmen who lobby for their interests. But who speaks for working families, the American lower middle class? They have no full-time leaders, no contemporary heroes. Occasionally, a public figure captures their imagination and begins to articulate or represent their problems. More often than not, however, he is addressing himself to their weaknesses rather than their strengths.

It is a sad commentary on American politics that Governor George Wallace has seemed to strike responsive chords in the working class. Agreed: there may be some bigotry and hatred in the hearts of working people. But, as the man seeking to give his son an apprenticeship noted, which of us is without some prejudice? There is also an enormous reservoir of compassion, good will, energy and longing for justice among those people that men like Governor Wallace do not attempt to reach or encourage.

A union leader in Connecticut told me in 1968 that many in his membership would have supported George Wallace but for one obstacle: listening to a Wallace speech, he said, did not make his men feel good; it made them feel remorse, as if they had sold out the values of human dignity in which they believed.

Vice-President Spiro Agnew is also said to be a spokesman for the workingman. President Nixon himself seeks to relate to working families. But these two leaders likewise only give working people scapegoats to dislike—TV networks, militant blacks and anarchistic college students—and very few positive reforms and accomplishments to improve their lives. Providing only scapegoats is smart politics because everyone knows the poor and the black and the young don't vote, but it clearly is not responsible politics for a country that faces a growing polarization between white working people and the rest of society. Our nation's leaders should try to unite—not divide.

Some political observers have noted that because blacks have nowhere to move but into the lower middle class, federal efforts should be directed at improving the white families' conditions. This thinking asserts that we will never solve the problems of blacks until we solve the problems of the lower middle class. For a time, I advocated that approach. Yet as I thought about it, I came to realize that it is not the right reason for helping the working white families. The deserving deserve assistance because they deserve it—not because somebody else is more deserving.

We should set out to help the lower middle class because it is the right thing to do, not because it will indirectly help blacks. We should help middle Americans because they are vitally important and essential to the success of this country, because this nation would collapse without them; because they erect our skyscrapers, dam our rivers, unload our ships, pave our roads, drive our trucks, police our streets, man our defenses; because they are the muscle and heart that keeps the country moving and because America needs them as much as they need America.

We can begin by making an agenda for action and basing it upon the problems that most seriously affect the working people. The major areas are jobs, housing, educational opportunities, health care and retirement.

Our basic goal should be to achieve full employment, so that workers can be confident that their jobs are secure. I have devoted a later chapter to actions

we must take to keep our economy strong and productive, particularly in light of our changing role in
the world economic community. We must also establish, however, the concept of the government as "employer of last resort" for men and women who have
lost or cannot find jobs in the private sector.

We face a great paradox in American society today: we have over 5 million unemployed men and
women in a country burdened with a huge backlog of
public service needs—in our parks and streets, slums
and countryside, schools and colleges, libraries, hospitals, nursing homes, public buildings—indeed,
throughout the public and nonprofit sectors of this
economy. The government as "employer of last resort" will ensure that all Americans are able to lead
meaningful, productive lives. A side effect will be
that tensions between white and black working people will ease as they begin to relax in the knowledge
that jobs exist for all who are willing and able to
work.

Another area of great conflict between blacks and
whites is housing. Lower-middle-class white Americans look at the economic walls shutting them out of
many suburbs and feel they are being left behind to
share what little they have with what they see as an
onrushing group of blacks who drive down housing
values wherever they go. Here, too, many working-

class whites look at housing programs that somehow never seem to apply to them.

For many years federal housing assistance was geared to public housing projects rather than individual home ownership. Lower-middle-class families were theoretically eligible for FHA and VA mortgage insurance programs, but higher housing costs have made it increasingly difficult for them to participate.

An average new home purchased in 1965 with an FHA-insured mortgage cost $16,800. Expenses for mortgage payments, taxes, insurance, utilities and maintenance and repairs came to approximately $147 per month. To build a similar house on a similar lot in 1970 would have cost about $24,500, with monthly payments of nearly $265, a 78 percent increase in the effective cost of buying and maintaining a new home in five years. A man earning less than $10,000 per year simply cannot afford these prices.

To fill the expanding cost-income gap, Congress passed in 1968 a subsidy program to assist low-income families wishing to purchase or rent decent housing. According to the Department of Housing and Urban Development, the typical family moving into a new home under this program in 1970 had an income of $6,200. The family usually had three children. The father, under thirty, often was employed as a fireman, teacher, or in some other service occupation. The average home purchased had a mortgage of $17,650, and the family received a federal subsidy of $80 per month to help cover the total monthly mortgage payment of $171.

The problem is that the homes the programs hope to build do not exist in sufficient numbers. Normally the mortgages under this new home ownership law are limited to $18,000 for a unit of up to three bedrooms. For a unit of four bedrooms or more for families of five or larger, the limitation is $21,000. In high-cost areas, these limits can be increased to $21,000 and $24,000 respectively. It is tough, if not impossible, to find a home at these prices, however. The median sales price of a new one-family home in America is $25,000. In the crowded Northeast, the cost is over $30,000. In fact, while 63 percent of the homes built in 1963 were priced under $20,000, only 34 percent now can be bought for that amount.

To make more housing available, our subsidy programs must be expanded by raising the ceilings on both income and price. Only then can working people feel confident that adequate housing at a reasonable price will always be available for them. This will raise the costs of the program dramatically, but these increases can be controlled if we open up the suburbs to more low- and moderate-income housing.

The same forces which have trapped the blacks in the inner cities have also limited the mobility of the white lower-middle-class Americans. They are now forced to compete with the blacks for the limited supply of affordable housing available. The lower middle class, therefore, has an equal stake in opening up the suburbs to low-income housing.

This nation must also adopt a program of national health insurance. I personally could get along without national health insurance. So could most of my colleagues in the House and Senate, for we have good insurance coverage. The nation's doctors don't have an overwhelming need for national health insurance, either. Nor do the people who run the hospitals and insurance programs. I have rarely heard doctors, hospital administrators or insurance executives complain too strongly about the cost of medical care in general or their own medical bills in particular. Americans who are rich don't have to worry about health costs, either.

Five million Americans, then, may find major sickness or injury an inconvenience or personal tragedy—but not a cause of bankruptcy. These fortunate Americans don't sweat out questions such as, should we pay the rent this month or the hospital? The grocer or the doctor? Is a sick child something we can afford this winter or next?

The fortunate Americans don't have to worry about collection agencies, hospital attorneys and bankruptcy court. They spend little time worrying over whether they will lose their health insurance if they are laid off during a rough economic period. More than 200 million Americans are not so lucky. These men and women, especially working-class Americans, are deeply afraid of the rising costs of medical care and the limitations of their own medical insurance.

For most families in this country, the symbol of medicine has become not the Red Cross or the physician's insigne but the dollar sign. The reasons behind this tragic situation are no secret. In the decade between 1960 and 1970, hospital costs almost tripled and doctors' fees nearly doubled. The average day in the hospital that cost $32.23 in 1960 cost $79.83 in 1970. The complete physical that cost $57 as recently as 1968 cost $100 in 1970.

If developments in health insurance had kept pace with the increases in cost, that would have relieved the problem significantly. But health insurance programs did not keep pace. In the face of rising costs, 24 million Americans still have no hospital insurance at all. That is one in every seven persons under the age of sixty-five. One in five Americans—or 35 million people—are without surgical insurance. These people want help. They want an end to the fear, the anxiety and the frustration of not knowing where their next antibiotic will come from. They need more comprehensive health insurance, and they need it in less complicated ways. They ask, if other countries can do this, why not the United States?

It is simple enough to say that everyone should have the right to receive care quickly and conveniently, that they should have the right not to worry about how it will be paid for, that they should have the right to be treated with dignity and respect. But it is not so easy to ensure those rights and devise the program that will succeed. It is an awesome, complex task.

A new national health program should be built upon these principles: (1) it should be essentially federally financed; (2) it should establish a system of universal entitlement, one program for the entire nation; (3) it should be open to everyone without exception; and (4) it should have no restrictions on the medical services that are covered or the length of time a person may receive the medical treatment he needs.

However, I am opposed to a national health insurance program totally dominated by the federal government. Instead of turning the whole effort over to the federal government or the private insurance industry, a wiser course would be to let each state make its own decision on how the program ought to be administered. The governor and the legislature would select whatever agency they wished to do the job. They could choose a Blue Cross carrier, a commercial company, a combination of the two, an existing state agency, or they could establish a semi-independent public corporation. The choice would be theirs. But the program would have to meet federal standards of entitlement, administration, cost control and quality control.

By allowing for regional variation and experimentation, by allowing for continual review and at least the possibility of someone else taking over the system, by allowing the health care issue to be politicized to a point where a governor would have to run for reelection on his administration of the program, concern for satisfying the consumer would be heightened.

It will take time to implement such a program. We should use that interval to work out the details in a series of pilot programs. Too often in this country, we have adopted major social programs with no idea whether they would work, or how they would work. We could have avoided much of the waste we now find in federal programs had we been willing at the start to admit our uncertainties and to start on a smaller scale.

Medical bills and unemployment are great burdens on working families. But the lack of higher educational opportunities for their children also troubles them. As a nation, we place a high premium on a college education, for example, but have not as yet guaranteed every American youngster the right to obtain his degree. Not every boy or girl should go to college, of course. Not every boy or girl is qualified. However, there are many dull-witted or uninterested children in well-to-do families who do go to college. Anyone who has attended college knows that brains and imagination are not essential qualities for the attainment of a degree.

Our goals should be to open the doors of our universities to all intelligent and interested youngsters, regardless of their parents' financial resources and to encourage those who, for one reason or another, are just filling up desk space to use their time more profitably. Academic ability is not a gift only the rich enjoy any more than an interest in nonacademic subjects is limited to the children of working people.

Our priorities are all wrong. Why should a young man who likes to work on cars be pressured by his parents to go to college when what he really wants to do is take a year of mechanical training at a vocational school and then go to work in an auto repair shop? My son had a friend whose parents insisted he go to college. The boy rebelled, moved to California and went to work servicing cars. Today he owns a chain of service stations.

My son and I have lost touch with the boy and his family. But when we knew them their chief concern was that mechanics have too little status in our society, so they wanted their son to do something that required a college degree. Never mind that the young man was good with his hands, was happiest handling wrenches and had no interest in conventional academic subjects. Had he not rebelled, he might have become an accountant or attorney and not been very happy or very good at it.

We should overcome the national obsession with college. People should recognize that good mechanics are as important to our society as competent lawyers. In fact, most of us can go through life rarely requiring the services of a lawyer. The same is not true of mechanics, plumbers and other skilled workmen without whose talents the country surely would literally collapse. By the same token, we must see to it that our colleges are open to the sons and daughters of working people.

We have begun compensatory and catch-up programs for the young men and women of the ghettos to enable them to go to college. Those programs are important and should be continued, improved and expanded. But no special effort is being made to bring working-class boys and girls into college. This annoys working-class parents, and they have a legitimate complaint. Consider their feeling when they hear of college programs in which ghetto blacks are admitted to colleges and receive tutoring and other benefits to help them meet academic standards. In most cases the standards are lowered to let them in. They are given scholarships or loans or jobs on or near the campus.

Compare that with the opportunities offered a working-class boy or girl. The young man's grades were quite ordinary in high school and, therefore, he cannot even get into the college. No effort is made to lower standards for him, even though his intellectual qualifications may be much higher than those of the ghetto black child. Even if the working-class boy is admitted, there are no special tutorial programs offered him. Nor are special scholarships, loans or jobs provided working-class youngsters to help them pay their own way. The point of this is not to criticize special treatment afforded poor blacks. It is simply to show the need for providing special help to working-class children if their families are ever going to believe that they are as important and deserving as anyone else.

The government's investment in the GI Bill and its educational benefits has been repaid many times over by the millions of veterans who have received assistance. Why not provide assistance to everyone qualified to attend college whose parents are unable to provide it themselves? For those with incomes between $5,000 and $15,000 it is frequently all but impossible to pay for a child's college expenses. Recent legislation has begun to move in this direction, but more must be done.

The federal government is also now spending over $500 million a year supporting vocational education programs. This figure should be increased as well. We should be building technical institutes across our land. This investment, too, will be returned to us manyfold. In large measure, this nation's wealth and preeminence in the world are the result of the technical know-how our people enjoy. American technical skill is famous throughout the world. We are great builders and earth-movers, if we are nothing else. Every youngster who does not go to college should have the opportunity to attend a vocational or technical school. There should be one or two in every metropolitan area with a population of 40,000 or 50,000. That school should function in response to the needs of the community in which it is located.

Finally, to help working-class Americans, we must

guarantee them a decent, reasonably comfortable, dignified retirement. If society is to be judged by the care it takes of its elderly members, American society is a failure. To be old in America is too often to be poor. Most working-class couples have seen their friends retire and find themselves living at or near the poverty level.

In 1969 the aged had less than half the income of those under age sixty-five. By December 1970, according to the Senate's Special Committee on Aging, approximately 5 million of the 20 million aged Americans lived in poverty, an incidence of poverty twice the rate of society generally. The number of those living in poverty decreased somewhat in recent years in this country for every group but older Americans. For them, the number rose.

Many of the aged poor are simply those who have been poor all their lives and have grown old. But an increasing number are working-class Americans who made enough while working to stay out of poverty but were unable to save much for retirement and find that pensions and Social Security have not kept them from growing into poverty.

This specter haunts many lower-middle-class Americans long before they reach age sixty-five. A new class of aging poor is being created. More workers are retiring before age sixty-five and accepting reduced Social Security benefits, not because they want to but because they have no choice. They are out of work, ill or engaged in marginal employment.

Widespread unemployment among workers who are over forty-five years old is increasing faster than in any other age group. This unemployment lasts longer than for younger workers, and the older person has greater difficulty in finding work at the same pay level after a prolonged layoff.

In addition to the over 1 million men and women over forty-five who are unemployed and seeking employment, more than 8 million males forty-five and older have totally withdrawn from the work force and are not reflected in unemployment statistics. Another 20 million women in this age category are also not in the labor force. Assuming that just 30 percent of the men and 10 percent of the women wanted and needed jobs—a conservative estimate made by the Senate's Special Committee on Aging—"real" unemployment for persons forty-five and older would approach 5.5 million people—500,000 more than the total statistical unemployment in the entire United States.

The federal government has ignored this plight of middle-aged people, contributing to some of the resentment felt by workers against a government that cares for the rich and attempts to provide for the

poor but ignores the average man. Less than 10 percent of the nation's manpower training and retraining efforts have focused on people forty-five and
older, notwithstanding their high unemployment.

The first thing we need to do is to ensure that those
on Social Security receive more adequate incomes. A
Social Security Administration study showed that
one-fourth of aged couples and two-fifths of single
beneficiaries receiving Social Security depended
solely on it for their entire support. At present, the
most a retired couple can receive is a little over $200
a month, and single or widowed persons receive a little more than half that. These figures are much too
low, as shown by the fact that 1.2 million Social
Security recipients are forced to rely on welfare as
well as Social Security for their subsistence. Congress
is considering increases in Social Security this year,
but hundreds of thousands of recipients will still have
to seek welfare help as well.

Some who object to significant increases in Social
Security argue that the program was never meant to
pay all the costs of retirement. That's true. But Social
Security is not a religion or a sacred ledger handed
down from on high. If it was not originally meant to
be a full retirement for the elderly, then let's change
it. All it takes is a majority of members of the Senate
and House and signature by the President and we

will have amended it sufficiently to enable every person in America to live out the last years of his or her life in reasonable comfort and dignity. This will require a larger investment in Social Security by working people, but I do not think they will mind if, at the same time, they understand that this will guarantee them a comfortable retirement.

As Social Security deductions are increased, however, the system should be made more equitable. Social Security taxes now are regressive, forcing lower-paid workers to pay a much higher percentage of their income than higher-paid employees. The injustice arises because everyone in Social Security is taxed 5.2 percent on their first $9,000 of earnings.

This formula is fine for Harry Smith, who makes $40,000 a year. His Social Security contribution comes to $468, or 1 percent of his total income. Smith has it made compared to Joe Taylor. Joe only made $9,000 this year, but he too pays $468. This is 5.2 percent of his salary, a rate five times greater than that paid by Smith. There is no justification for this difference. Social Security should be reformed so that everyone pays a more reasonable share of their income and receives more adequate benefits.

Another inequity for the working class in the Social Security system is the limitation on income by Social Security pensioners. Many elderly persons are eager to work and help support themselves. But the government discourages work by penalizing them for every dollar earned above $1,680 a year.

Consider a widow on Social Security. She may receive $150 a month from Social Security. She takes a job that pays her $3,600 a year. For every two dollars she earns over $1,680 and up to $2,880, a dollar in Social Security benefits is lost. Above $2,880 she loses benefits on a dollar-for-dollar basis. This limitation applies until the age of seventy-two, when she will be allowed to work as often as she likes without losing Social Security benefits.

The effect of this earnings limitation penalizes the working class. While our working widow is losing benefits for every dollar earned, our friend Smith is allowed on retirement to receive all of his income from investments, stocks, bonds, copyrights, patents, rentals, dividends and other pensions without losing a penny of Social Security benefits, even if his outside income is $100,000. Two million elderly workers meanwhile are losing some or all of their Social Security benefits for which they paid a higher percentage of their salaries. This is wrong and must be changed if Social Security is to be a program that meets the needs of the lower middle class. Proposals are pending now to raise the income ceiling; but, again, this is only a start in the right direction.

Social Security is not the sole means of providing for the retirement of our citizens. Approximately $140 billion is now invested in 34,000 private pension funds covering 30 million workers. Unfortunately, more than half of the private work force are not employed by a company or union that has a pension plan. As many as half of those workers who have a plan may not receive pension benefits when they retire and more than half of all persons who will receive private pension benefits will receive less than $1,000 a year.

The fine print in many pension plans rivals those famous life insurance policies that, once you get through the disclaimers, covered you against being run over by a herd of buffalo in downtown Detroit. Many pension plans provide no benefits for widows or widowers, require years of work before a worker has a right to any pension and cause him to forfeit all rights if he changes jobs. As a New York *Times* survey showed last year, private pension plans are "a phantom for millions of workers who never collect them."

We are slowly becoming aware of this problem. Proposals have been made to allow workers to transfer their interest in one pension plan to another when they change jobs, to shorten the years of work necessary to qualify for pension rights and to give tax de-

ductions to those investing in pension plans for themselves or their employees.

These proposals all move in the right direction. A
simpler idea has been suggested by Ralph Nader.
Each employee would be responsible for arranging
his own retirement plan. His employer would make
payments to a fund chosen by the employee, who
could transfer his interest at any time. The funds
would therefore compete in the open market place to
provide better benefits. The government would set
minimum standards for all funds and would provide
insurance to avoid the increasing problem of pension
fund failures.

All of these suggestions deserve consideration and
support. Whatever we do, we must help workers to
ensure that their retirement years will not be years of
poverty and insecurity.

That is my proposed agenda for action to improve
the economics and quality of life for working Americans. I don't pretend to have all the answers for these
very complicated problems and have only briefly described what I feel are solutions to the major problem areas.

A final item remains on my agenda for action. No
Congress and no government can achieve it without
the people's support. I would like to suggest that we
alter the tone and style of our public and private dis-

cussions about our most pressing problems. We should raise our level of tolerance for the ideas and proposals of those with whom we disagree. We should stop talking only to those with whom we agree and try to put ourselves in the shoes of others.

As the decade of the sixties wore on, the level of public and private discussion in this country hit rock bottom. Obscenities punctuated too many sentences. Thoughtful, considered opinions were replaced by stormy assertions and bullying tactics, many of them directed at and returned by the working class. As a result, a good number of American working men and women who once thought of themselves as tolerant, progressive, understanding citizens of a great nation now are having second thoughts about a lot of things. Why be tolerant, they ask, when progress seems to help those beneath us and those above but never us? Why be understanding of the problems of others? Who is trying to understand our problems?

Protest is important. People should work and fight for their rights. But we ultimately will rise or fall together, and this means that no element of our society can be ignored, forgotten or downgraded.

VI

Welfare and Poverty

IF WORDS WERE DOLLARS, poverty would not exist in America. Talk is cheap, and as far as the poor are concerned, meaningless. Amid all the deep discussions and complex theories about poverty, the poor—all 26 million of them—have heard plenty of big talk about what is going to be done to help them. Yet they are still poor. They are remarkably patient. They simply wait around while the government and its one-hundred-dollar-a-day consultants define and redefine the poor, their plight, how they got that way, who is to blame and what the alternatives are for leading them out of poverty.

Jules Feiffer drew a perceptive characterization of the word game we play with the poor. Portrayed was an old, penniless man soliloquizing in a rocking chair. He observed: "I used to think I was poor. Then they told me I wasn't poor. I was needy. Then they told me it was self-defeating to think of myself as needy. I was deprived. Then they told me deprived was a bad image. I was underprivileged. Then they told me underprivileged was overused. I was disadvantaged. I still don't have a dime. But I have a great vocabulary."

The Feiffer cartoon underscores my contention that we have studied poverty and the poor long enough. It is time we recognized that the poor are poor because they do not have enough money. Yet we have given them everything but money. We have offered them job training. But at the end of the training there is rarely a job. We offer them services: social services, legal services, nutrition services, health services, educational deprivation services, family planning services, housing services. We have presumed to make decisions ourselves as to what 26 million impoverished Americans need.

We have deluded ourselves into believing that we are giving the poor control of their own destinies by allowing them "maximum feasible participation" in these many service programs. What we have really done is impose on the poor our ideas of what is good for them. Then we have allowed them to participate within those definitions of what we believe to be proper. In essence, welfare as presently structured acts as an elite decision-making process, as undemocratic as it is arrogant. "Maximum feasible participation" is actually no more than maximum feasible manipulation.

It's not just a question of needing to spend more money on poverty programs. According to the principal antipoverty bureau in Washington, the Office of Economic Opportunity (OEO), over 168 programs in the federal government are designed to eliminate poverty. In fiscal 1972 these programs will cost the taxpayers $31 billion. Despite that expenditure, 26 million Americans still live in poverty, and the number is increasing.

If we distributed the $31 billion we now spend to end poverty directly to those 26 million Americans, every poor family of four would receive $4800, $900 above the poverty level. Taking only $11 billion of the $31 billion and giving it to the poor would bring every poor family in America up to the poverty level when added to the money they already receive.

I am not proposing that we dismantle all our poverty programs. But 168 separate programs are far too many. A large number of them could be ended to-morrow, and the only complaints voiced would come not from the poor but from the bureaucrats running the 168 programs.

The government, the public, the recipients them-selves, everyone seems agreed that welfare as now handled is a failure and that reform is required. But reform for reform's sake will not bring sanity to our welfare efforts. We must first reach some consensus about what we want to achieve with welfare. Do we want to assist the poor—or don't we? The answer is in doubt.

As a people, we cannot make up our minds just how we feel about poverty. On the one hand, we are a compassionate and generous people. On the other, we resent welfare programs in general, suspect that most recipients are cheaters or lazy or both and are convinced that with some added effort recipients could pull themselves up by their bootstraps and buy a home in the suburbs.

This contradiction in the American civilization about poverty—a compassion for the destitute cou-pled with a belief that the destitute got themselves into that predicament—was reflected in a 1971 Har-ris public opinion survey that showed 85 percent of those polled expressed grave concern that some Americans suffer from hunger. Yet 82 percent believed that if the hungry people showed a little more get-up-and-go the hunger problem would be solved. A 1964 Harris poll revealed that 68 percent of those interviewed agreed the government should guarantee that no one be without food, clothing and shelter. Yet the same poll reported that most people felt welfare and relief recipients were lazy. The suspicion that welfare recipients are cheaters is not a new one. It goes back to Depression days. In 1936, 24 percent of those polled thought that persons taken off relief would have an easy time finding work.

Inevitably, the popular belief that welfare recipients could find work if they really wanted to became structured into the welfare program itself. Welfare investigators were hired. Their mission was to ferret out the chiselers and save the taxpayers' money. The assumption sometimes seems to be that people on welfare are a group of fun-loving swingers who spend their mornings sleeping late, their afternoons at the track and their evenings at wild parties. Welfare recipients are said to be enjoying this jet-set kind of existence because permissive government officials will not crack down on them and make them go to work.

The myth of the lazy, cheating welfare recipient has several flaws. First, people generally misunderstand who receives welfare assistance from the federal government. Just who are these unsavory characters who, from the sanctuary of the handout line, rob us blind? Well, some of them are actually blind —that is to say, 1 percent of the 13 million welfare recipients have lost their eyesight or were born blind and qualify for federal assistance. Another 15 percent of the welfare recipients are the elderly. A little more than 10 percent are either totally and permanently disabled or incapacitated and must stay at home. Fifty-five percent are dependent children and 18 percent are mothers. That comes to nearly 99 percent of all recipients on relief rolls.

Only about 1 percent of those receiving welfare are able-bodied men who could work, no one having yet proposed that the aged, blind, disabled and children be required to work. One percent of 13 million is about 130,000. Putting at least that many men to work and off relief is a goal we should strive for. These recipients should be removed from the welfare rolls if—and this is a vital *if*—they are offered employment and reject it.

The fact of the matter is that many, if not most, of these 130,000 men would like to have jobs. A government-sponsored study showed 80 percent of these adults wanted to work and almost half of them are already enrolled in voluntary training programs. This is hardly the picture of millions of slackers making a full-time job out of avoiding work.

Of the 2.6 million welfare mothers, between 70
and 80 percent of them would also like to work if
jobs were available. Some 14 percent of these women
already work and 7 percent are in work training. Another 35 percent could work if adequate day-care
programs were available for their children. Five percent would have employment potential following extensive social rehabilitation efforts and the remaining
40 percent have little employment potential because
they care for small children at home or have major
physical or mental incapacities or other insurmountable work barriers. Even with these barriers the great
majority want to work.

What adults on welfare lack is not the incentive to
work but the opportunity to work. There are not
enough jobs to go around in our society. Five million
Americans are unemployed. Skilled workmen are out
of work in our nation. Engineers and physicists cannot find jobs. Why do we assume the very poor and
unskilled can land jobs when others above them on
the socioeconomic ladder are having so much difficulty?

Even those working and not on the federal welfare
rolls are not necessarily very well off today in our society. You don't have to be unemployed to live in
poverty. The sad fact is that millions of Americans
work full-time and still have subpoverty wages. Forty

percent of the people living in poverty are in families headed by a full-time worker.

The myth about millions of welfare cheaters does not hold up much better than the one about all those loafers. Suspected incidents of fraud or misrepresentation among welfare recipients occur in less than four-tenths of 1 percent of the total welfare caseload. No more than 5 or 6 percent are technically ineligible because of a misunderstanding of the rules, agency mistakes or changes in family circumstances not yet reflected in payment checks.

Many publicized charges of cheating or ineligibility simply have not stood up under investigation. The true facts, however, did not receive the same attention as the original charges. The news media widely reported in December 1970, for example, that 22 percent of the Nevada welfare caseload was found ineligible by that state. A follow-up investigation by the federal government showed that the ineligibility was only in the 3 percent range. In New York City it was widely reported in 1971 that 18 percent of the assistance recipients failed to make a personal appearance to claim their welfare checks as required under a new law, leaving the impression that those 18 percent were fraudulently on the welfare rolls. Again, a follow-up investigation showed that legitimate reasons unrelated to fraud existed for failure to claim the payments for all but a small minority of the 18 percent.

Welfare fraud is, if anything, much less prevalent than the white-collar fraud of income-tax cheating and expense-account conniving. Tax evasion seems to be more socially acceptable than welfare fraud, even though it invariably involves more money than welfare cheating. In a recent tax case, for example, a prominent Southern physician was convicted of tax evasion and given a jail term by a federal district court in the doctor's hometown. Almost immediately, 30 other local doctors filed amended tax returns, all of them showing more income and fewer deductions than previously reported.

While the proportion of welfare recipients who deliberately falsify information is very low, we should take the necessary steps to detect such fraud and deal with it accordingly. But in doing so we must not ignore the legitimate needs of the 95 percent on welfare through no fault or failing of their own.

But some argue that the failing is their own. If not loafers or cheaters, those on welfare at least are there because of problems of desertion or illegitimacy. This myth often takes the form of accusing welfare mothers of having children for the sole purpose of increasing their welfare checks.

First, regarding desertion. The facts behind the

myth are not that fathers feel no responsibility to their wives and children and desert at the first chance, thereby making them burdens of society. In some cases that may be true. But all too often the grim reality is that our welfare system as now structured encourages the disintegration of the family unit, and virtually forces fathers out of their homes.

In most states a mother with children can receive welfare benefits only if there is no man present in the house. If the husband is unemployed or making a substandard wage, his only choice for the financial good of his family is to desert, thereby making the family eligible for welfare. Desertion is not a "cause" of the welfare mess but rather the "effect" of a poorly structured system.

The companion problem of illegitimacy, which bothers many Americans, also should be placed in its proper perspective. The facts are that most children on welfare were born before their mothers began to receive assistance. The average welfare family has only three children, slightly above the national average for all Americans. In the last few years the trend has been toward smaller families on welfare since the birth rate in welfare families, like the birth rate for the general population, is dropping. While a certain proportion of welfare children are illegitimate, we should also recognize that as many as one-third of all firstborn children in this country are conceived out of wedlock.

The typical payment for an additional child on welfare, $35 a month, does not provide any financial incentive. This sum does not cover the cost of rearing a young child, nor does it buy many luxuries for a mother.

Finally, welfare mothers know better than anyone that added children in a welfare family only mean added heartbreak. Consider these sad vignettes pieced together in the Hartford area by Hartford *Courant* reporter Barbara Carlson.

Mrs. Garcia is a welfare mother. She is a thirty-three-year-old Puerto Rican. She has eight children, the oldest thirteen, the youngest three. She was three months pregnant when her husband was killed in an accident at work. Mrs. Garcia was promised compensation, but she never received it. So she moved from her small village in Puerto Rico to Hartford. She was, she explained, "looking for something better." Something better was a shabby $180-a-month apartment in Hartford and the prospect of a cold New England winter while her children are still wearing clothes from their warm homeland.

Mrs. Henry is a welfare mother. She was deserted by her husband after her twins were born. She is a tall, attractive black woman, twenty-six years old.

Her $140-a-month apartment is attractively furnished. Besides her twin sons, Mrs. Henry has two other boys, six and three years old. The three-year-old undergoes treatment in a hospital. He does not talk, is hyperactive and has an eye turned in. Mrs. Henry has not lost hope. "I've had a lot of downfalls in my life," she says, "so I'm not going to grow old here. . . . I can't sit around and cop out on my kids. I'm not going to have them have a lack of education. They didn't ask to be born."

Mrs. Harrison is a welfare mother. She is a thirty-four-year-old divorcee with six children. A European by birth, she married a man from Hartford, and they settled there. She has been divorced only a month. Her children all suffer from emotional or physical problems. "My mother sent me $3.00 for Christmas," Mrs. Harrison recalls. "She doesn't realize it won't get anywhere here. She works hard for a living. She cleans house. She has nothing extra. We never had nothing." Mrs. Harrison's eight-year-old son, Bobby, is "very touchy," she says. Bobby plays with matches and won't talk about his father. He still needs special help, his mother says, "but his writing and reading are good. He got 100 in a class, so I bought him some gloves. They were a dollar at Bradlee's."

These women—none of their real names were

used—received assistance from the Connecticut State Welfare Department under the federally sponsored Aid to Families with Dependent Children (AFDC) program. They are neither typical nor untypical. The only thing they have in common is hardship and the fact that the husband is gone. In fact, a typical welfare family does not exist. Each family and each member of it has his or her own hopes, fears and problems.

It is easy enough to say that these mothers should cart their kids off to day-care centers, go to work and go off public assistance. But day-care centers in most communities throughout the nation are limited in number, location and capabilities. Hartford, for example, has eight centers with a total capacity of 550. All but one of the centers is located in one section of town and only three accept children older than five. Almost no facilities are available for infants under the age of three. The truth of the matter is that day-care centers, at least as they are presently organized, are not even a partial solution to the problems of the welfare mother. These women often cannot go to work because their children come first. That is the way it should be.

It is a myth, therefore, that the welfare rolls are riddled with cheaters, bums and loafers. But that isn't the only myth about welfare. There are many more.

Foremost among them is the assumption that, inadequate as welfare may be, everybody who needs help is receiving some form of assistance. I wish it were true. But it isn't. Single people and childless couples, for example, receive no federal assistance whatsoever in the fifty states. The destitute are better off in America if they are married and have children. There is no logic to that.

Millions of other Americans live on next to nothing who have never heard of welfare—or if they have heard of it, have no idea of how to apply for it. They may be illiterate or retarded or suffer from another handicap that isolates them from the necessary information about welfare.

Other misconceptions about welfare abound. Another frequently stated assertion which does not hold up under examination is that welfare is a payoff to black people, the assumption being that most welfare recipients are black. That is not true. A high percentage of families on welfare are black, to be sure, a tragic 46 percent. But white families constitute the largest group—49 percent—of all welfare recipients. Most of the remaining 5 percent are American Indians and other minorities.

Lots of welfare recipients drive around in Cadillacs, have color TV sets and just live it up in general. Right? Sorry, wrong again. According to the Bureau of Labor Statistics, a family of four needs a monthly income of $458 to live at a minimally adequate level of health and nutrition. The state of New Jersey, the most generous provider of welfare benefits of all the fifty states, gives $341 a month to a family of four, $117 beneath the basic minimal standard. There are not many Cadillacs and color TVs on that budget—even if the kids are not eating.

Which raises another notion—that welfare mothers buy a lot of liquor and other personal things and, in so catering to their own desires, neglect the needs of their children. A survey of welfare mothers released by the Department of Health, Education and Welfare in 1971 showed, to the contrary, that they are deeply concerned about their youngsters' needs and wish they had more money to devote to them.

Seventy-seven percent of the welfare mothers interviewed said that if they had more money they would spend it on food and clothes for the kids. Forty-two percent pointed out they relied on used clothes to help make ends meet. Seventeen percent said they occasionally kept their children home from school because they lacked decent clothes and shoes. Another 10 percent said they would spend additional welfare funds on moving to a better home or apartment.

No mother wants to see her children go hungry and suffer constant illness. But poverty and poor health go hand in hand, reinforcing each other in a vicious cycle which assures generational dependence on welfare. The cycle often begins with a pregnant mother living in poverty, although not necessarily on welfare, being forced to eat a nutritionally inadequate diet, having to choose starchy, filling foods over meat and eggs and vegetables. If she is like at least 50 percent of the impoverished pregnant women in this country, she receives no prenatal medical care.

The child born to such a woman has twice as great a chance of dying in his first year of life as the average newborn baby. If he lives he faces the possibility that poor prenatal nutrition has already hindered his brain development. During his early childhood years the protein deficiencies in his diet can further retard his brain and body growth. Like 50 percent of the children living in poverty, he will not receive adequate immunization and, like two-thirds of the children of the poor, he will never see a dentist.

The only chance for a welfare child to break out of poverty—through a decent education—will be very small. His mental and physical growth will probably already be stunted before he reaches school, and he will probably be listless, unable to concentrate and angry at a society which provides so well for so many, yet ignores him.

He and the children of other poor families will have shorter life spans and four times more nervous disorders and mental illnesses than the population at large. He will suffer three times as many orthopedic ailments and eight times as many visual defects as the average American.

He will then go out into the world with three strikes against him and be expected to pull himself up by his bootstraps. With poor health and inadequate education he will either find no jobs open to him or be employed at subpoverty wages. In sum, he can't pull himself up by his bootstraps because, even if he has boots, more likely than not he will not have the strength to pull.

We will break this cycle only if we are willing to spend the money needed to raise the standards of living of the millions in this country living in poverty. But thus far our response has been more money for more programs and experts, not more money for the poor.

The middlemen—not the poor—are moving forward in the economy as a result of the war on poverty. Former OEO Director Donald Rumsfeld has estimated that 2 million people are employed by federal, state and local governments to administer programs to aid the 26 million poor. In addition, there are scores of former antipoverty officials, and hundreds of private management consulting firms they go to work for are living off the poor. There is big money in poverty—big money for everybody, that is, except the poor. Since OEO was established six years ago, for example, some $600 million has been spent on contracts to private consulting firms for consultation, evaluation, technical assistance and support, including forty-four evaluations of Project Head Start.

In 1970, OEO was paying on 128 consultation, evaluation, technical assistance and support contracts worth $56.7 million. Thirty-two of these contracts worth $11.5 million were held by sixteen companies which had thirty-five former OEO officials working for them. At least 254 firms were found to have received $100,000 or more in OEO contracts. Of these, 127 have headquarters or branch offices in the Washington, D.C., area.

As one poverty worker confided in me, "I have no illusions, Senator. I'm in poverty for the money." This young man was making more money than he had ever made in his life.

The poverty industry was born in the 1960s. It was then that we recognized for the first time the size and seriousness of poverty in America. To combat poverty on a mass scale was a noble effort and neither Presidents Kennedy nor Johnson should be faulted for their good intentions. But where they failed—where all of us involved failed—was in not insisting on pretesting all programs, in not evaluating their effectiveness and, most important, in forgetting the simple truth that poor people need, first and foremost, money.

I speak with some experience here. I am the first to admit that I placed too much emphasis on poverty programs when I was Secretary of the Department of Health, Education and Welfare in 1961 and 1962 under President Kennedy. At my confirmation hearing, I pledged myself to extensive reform of the nation's public assistance efforts. Shortly thereafter, I wrote a memorandum to the Commissioner of Social Security, who was responsible for administering welfare at that time. In that memo, I said that "too much emphasis has been placed on just getting an assistance check into the hands of an individual. If we are ever going to move constructively in this field, we must come to realize that our efforts must involve a variety of helpful services, of which giving a money payment is only one."

This chapter was not meant to be the "confessions of a former Secretary of HEW," but a fundamental lesson can be drawn from my own experience. It is that the 1960s were blessed with an abundance of good intentions. But too many of them went awry.

What we must not do in the 1970s is wed ourselves to the errors of the past just because we don't want to admit we were wrong back then.

Today, ten years later, it is clear that our antipoverty efforts failed. The philosophy of the 1960s—to provide a vast array of services to the poor—must be judged by results. There are 26 million poor Americans. They suffer from malnutrition, lack of clothing, inadequate housing—not because they lack social services, advice and counseling but because they lack money, the great equalizer. As the Jules Feiffer character said, the poor still don't have a dime—but they have great vocabularies.

Our society has fulfilled its promises to millions of Americans and as a result we are a wealthy nation. But as the perquisites of citizenship have increased, so, too, have our responsibilities to society and our fellow man. As a nation we can no longer tolerate a system of public assistance which fails to meet the most basic principles of dignity, adequacy and equity.

We begin by recognizing that the best way to help the poor is to give them direct cash payments. We are a nation of limited resources and of limited ability to correct the injustices of poverty overnight. Someday we may find out how to eliminate poverty. Until then, we can better serve the needs of the poor by providing them with money and letting them make their own decisions about how they want to spend it. They can do no worse than we have done.

For example, a family of four with an income of less than $3,945 is deemed by present standards to be living in poverty. Our goal should be to give that family the amount of money needed to bring its income up to at least $3,945. Then that family will be out of poverty. The money should continue on a sliding scale until the family is able to earn enough to pay its own way.

Those who agree with me in principle will ask where additional funds will come from to make direct cash payments to the poor. As I noted earlier, we now have 168 poverty programs spending over $30 billion dollars a year, the equivalent of $4,800 for every poor family of four. If necessary, some of those programs can be abolished and the money distributed directly.

Howls of protest will be heard, but we have a sorry record in many of those programs. Conditions in Appalachia, for example, dramatize the inability of our poverty programs to get money to the poor. A decade ago, the coal counties of West Virginia, eastern Kentucky and western Virginia—the core of Appalachia —were on the brink of disaster. Tens of thousands of idle miners and their families faced starvation.

Struck by the hardship he witnessed in this region while campaigning for President, John Kennedy promised a new era for Appalachia. President Johnson vowed to continue the effort. Great sums were appropriated—over $2 billion for Appalachia—but today, a decade later, the million or so impoverished whites of Appalachia remain rooted in poverty and political impotence. Our programs in Appalachia won a battle or two. But the war is being lost, because only the generals seem to be prospering.

Homer Bigart, of the New York *Times,* found that a visitor to the region saw signs of affluence in the towns and cities of Appalachia. There was money in the towns, he wrote. The merchants, the doctors, the lawyers and the courthouse politicians had been enriched by the inflow of federal funds. But in the backwoods and hollows, life seemed as wretched as ever. Many families still live in cabins with no water supply and no sewage facilities except privies that often empty directly into streams. The threat of hunger persists.

Bigger Social Security payments, black-lung benefits and a vastly expanded food-stamp program have enabled Appalachian poor people to stave off hunger and to subsist in cheerless deprivation. Yet thousands of families lack even enough money for food stamps. And the school lunch program, which provides free or reduced-price lunches to needy children, does not reach thousands of children who need it.

Poverty programs are not the only area in which substantial revenues can be found. The Department of the Treasury estimates that special tax benefits and subsidies principally of advantage to the rich cost the American taxpayers over $40 billion a year. Much of this revenue, as well as funds wasted in programs ranging from farm subsidies to unnecessary defense expenditures, could be more profitably applied to a program of direct payments to the poor. If nothing else, we should put our "welfare" programs for the rich in better perspective by taking Herbert Gans's suggestion and relabeling all of our subsidies and tax loopholes with more realistic names—the "Oil Producers' Public Assistance Program," "Tobacco Growers' Dole," "Aid to Sick and Dependent Airlines," and "Tax Relief for Purchasers of Tax-Exempt Bonds."

Direct payment to the poor, or a "guaranteed annual income," is not a radical proposal. It once was. But no more. Not since President Nixon endorsed it. It is an irony of history that a Republican President, adjudged by his liberal critics as too conservative and unresponsive to the needs of the have-nots of our society, should be the first Chief Executive to propose a radical departure from the conventional welfare system.

Unfortunately, President Nixon was not candid

with the American people about this. Instead, he presented his proposal for welfare reform, the "Family Assistance Program," or FAP, as it came to be called, by stressing the need to support the "work ethic" in this country and to get the loafers and cheaters off the welfare rolls. In short, he chose to emphasize and reinforce the myths of welfare that he knew and we already have seen are unfounded in fact. The result was not the conservative support for welfare reform the President sought but more confusion about who was on welfare and what the President was proposing to do for them.

Nonetheless, while the amount proposed—and perhaps passed by now—$2,400 a year for a family of four—was well below the poverty level of $3,945, the principal was there: the President had proposed a guaranteed minimum annual income—very minimum—but guaranteed nonetheless. With all of its failings, FAP is the beginning of the end to welfare as we have known it for so long and the start of a more enlightened, humane and efficient system.

The President's program has two facets: improvement of existing federal welfare programs, primarily covering those who cannot work; and extension of federal assistance to the "working poor" for the first time. Unfortunately, this distinction was not clearly set forth. Therefore, when I suggested early this year that we try pilot programs for the working poor before starting this new program, the immediate assumption was that I was talking about piloting everything the President was suggesting. I ended up talking personally with the President about this, press conferences were held and editorials written before the dust had finally settled.

The President finally agreed with me that pilot programs made "good sense." As I have discussed elsewhere, our social programs often failed in the past because we adopted huge national programs before we had any assurances that they would work. When they failed, those in need became further disillusioned, and social progress was set back, since opponents of change were provided strong arguments for doing little or nothing to solve our basic problems.

At first glance the solution to the problems of the working poor is simple: Pay them the minimum wage. Unfortunately, the federal minimum of $1.60 an hour provides a gross annual salary of only $3,200—$700 less than the poverty level for a family of four. Congress is considering raising the minimum wage; but, even if it were adequate, it would not protect everyone. Today almost 12 million workers in the private sector are not covered by the minimum wage, including almost 7 million workers in small retail and service establishments, over half a million workers on farms, and over 2 million domestics.

A more difficult problem is developing a program designed to ensure that those who work are better off working rather than receiving welfare and sitting at home. Under the income supplement program proposed by the President, workers making less than the minimum guaranteed by the federal government would receive income supplements so that it would always be more profitable to work than simply to receive welfare. The concept seems sound, and I support it. But the novelty, scope and cost of this approach dictate that it be tried out on a pilot basis before being implemented on a national basis.

Other failings in the President's program are substantial. While FAP has already passed the House and is pending at this writing in the Senate, I am certain that any bill passed this year will leave undone much that needs to be done. Amendments I have proposed, for instance, would start benefit payments the first year for a family of four at $3,000, $600 above the President's proposal. More important, my amendments would establish a national goal to end poverty by 1976, our nation's two-hundredth anniversary, by raising benefit levels to the poverty level by that year.

By that same date, the federal government should

have taken over from the states and local governments all costs of welfare. We have heard much talk of revenue sharing, but no program would relieve more of the present financial strain from the states and cities than taking the welfare burden off their backs. Individual cities and states should not be required to administer or fund this nation's welfare program. No city or state is responsible for generating its welfare population. If the economy of this country is unable to provide adequate support for its citizens, the nation as a whole should undertake the responsibility of meeting their needs.

We must also ensure that all the poor come within the scope of our federal welfare program. Early in his administration, President Nixon expressed concern for the forgotten Americans in this country. The forgotten people of his welfare proposals are the 1.8 million persons under age sixty-five in families without children and the 2.3 million single persons who live in poverty, none of whom are eligible for public assistance under FAP.

The incidence of poverty reaches the highest levels among persons not connected with a family unit. Some 561,000 have no cash income at all. Moreover, it makes no sense to deny assistance to a couple without children and provide $2,000 to a couple with one child. Childless couples and single men and women in need have as much right as anyone to assistance and should be given it.

The President's original proposal stressed the need to train able-bodied welfare recipients to work, but it provided no jobs for these men and women at the end of the training. And this is at a time when unemployment had become one of the country's most serious problems. In 1970, Oklahoma's Senator Fred Harris and I were able to get the administration to provide for the creation of 30,000 public service jobs. This year's version upped the figure to 200,000, but even this is only a beginning.

No "make-work" program is needed. The visible deterioration of our cities, environment and health services makes it clear that much needs to be done in public service at the state and local level. It is estimated that local governments could easily use 3 million to 4 million more employees to provide basic services. Public service jobs can provide meaningful work in such fields as health, social services, public safety, environmental protection, urban and rural development, welfare, recreation and education. We should also authorize jobs in the field of criminal justice to provide much-needed personnel in tasks such as bail procedures, parole and probation, corrections, halfway houses and juvenile homes.

Guaranteeing jobs by itself will not begin to make

employment a meaningful concept for many of those on welfare. The day-care facilities of this country are woefully inadequate, and the President's veto in late 1971 of the comprehensive day-care program, together with the inadequate day-care provisions of FAP, only undercut efforts to provide work for those on welfare. More day-care services are needed and must be provided for everyone who needs them in this country, not just the poor.

All of this will cost money. But to save money on welfare we have to spend money—money to provide a system that opens opportunity for this generation's welfare children to become the next generation's productive citizens—money to bring millions of Americans out of misery and hopelessness, which is a daily fact of life in tenements and shacks throughout the nation.

The poor live in a different world than the members of affluent America, but their awareness, hopes and aspirations are the same as those of society as a whole. Through the media—newspapers, magazines, radio and television—they are acutely aware of the standard which most of us take for granted. They seek the same quality of education and the same level of achievement we all do. The difference lies in the possibility of realizing their hopes and dreams. For them, there is no hope. The American dream to the poor is still one long nightmare.

Ultimately, we must be willing to admit that welfare is a confession of our society's failures in education, employment and housing. We presently spend less than 1.5 percent of our trillion-dollar economy on welfare and less than 5 percent of government spending at all levels. Even the 2 percent or 3 percent of our economy I propose to spend for welfare is a small overhead to pay for the failures of our system. We can afford to do no less.

VII

The Individual in
Society

WE ARE A NATION that believes wholeheartedly in
the worth of the individual and his right to map out
his own destiny, make his own luck and influence the
decisions of his own government. This belief is
deeply embedded in our history, our folklore and our
image of ourselves. Our past is replete with men and
women who set out to overcome great adversity and
did just that. Our forefathers conquered a continent
and tamed a frontier. We would do the same.

The very word "frontier" has a special significance
to us. It symbolizes individuals—not organized, dis-

ciplined armies—but individuals on their own against rugged terrain, extreme weather, unknown enemies and other dangers. Alaskans call their state "the last frontier" and President John Kennedy's inauguration launched "the new frontier."

In the folk imagination, the frontier is tough, risky and daring. It is no place for faint hearts and weak backs. It is the Wright brothers, in 1903, airborne for the first time—and it is Neil Armstrong planting his country's flag on the lunar surface. The frontier is individuals doing things.

But the frontiers are no longer as well defined as they once were. We are no longer as confident of our abilities to control our own destinies as individuals. Where once open spaces and untrammeled freedom existed we now find cluttered cities and huge impersonal institutions that seem to control our every move. For many Americans, ours has become an organization-oriented society.

In the past forty years, for example, while our population has increased by two-thirds, federal employment has multiplied by a factor of five and the federal budget has increased by a factor of sixty-five. In the last twenty years, the number of state and local employees has more than doubled. Universities now are the size of cities with 25,000 to 40,000 students. The largest 500 corporations control almost 75 percent of the assets of American business.

The age of bureaucracy and technology has left people confused and disillusioned about their roles as individuals. Americans complain of anonymity. They feel voiceless and powerless before impersonal forces they do not understand, forces which are new to the American experience. Everything is so big—big government, big business, big labor, big department stores, big universities, big newspapers and television networks—while the individual citizen, by contrast, seems to have shrunk in importance.

The legacy of this organizational growth is the increasing distrust Americans have of their institutions. The Center of Political Studies of Michigan's Institute for Social Research reported in 1971 that the proportion of those professing to have a high degree of trust in the federal government had dropped from 62 percent to 37 percent in six years. Lou Harris reported later in the year that "sizable majorities of the public are prepared to believe the worst about politicians." Eighty-one percent believe politicians promise one thing and do another. Some 63 percent believe "most politicians are in politics to make money for themselves." And 59 percent believe "most politicians take graft."

Harris earlier found other institutions in this country did not fare much better. In five years, the number of Americans who have confidence in the major institutions in this country—churches, corporations, the federal government, the armed services, television networks and newspapers—had dropped to less than 30 percent for each institution.

As the credibility of institutions is questioned, the nation faces this dilemma: How do we take an idea we nourished in the eighteenth century—democracy—and give it life in a twentieth-century world? How do we preserve individual worth, freedom and identity in a world of technology, large-scale organizations and impersonal bureaucracies? How shall we provide a voice for each man in the vital decisions that affect his life?

The answer will not be found in bemoaning the death of town-meeting government and the loss of smaller and more manageable institutions. We cannot return to the days of open spaces and towns of 5,000 to 10,000. Nor can we break up every industry into fifty or more active competitors or cut federal expenditures in half.

But we can restructure our existing institutions and create new ones to give the individual a larger role in the decisions affecting his life. When in doubt, we should opt in favor of more participation—not less. More citizen involvement will not necessarily speed things up. But speed is not the sole issue.

In our quest for efficiency, centralization and the avoidance of controversy, we rob people of much of the substance of life. Too many decisions are made for them. The lack of personal participation and responsibility generates a malaise and disaffection with life, and it deprives the institutions in our society of views and information they need. Knowledge and wisdom are not the preserve of a handful of leaders. The people often know better than any institution what's good for them.

No institutions affect our daily lives more than the governments we elect and the private-enterprise system we support. With both, the individual has begun to feel an inability to accomplish anything. He cannot make his voice heard. It is here, therefore, that we should begin reform.

Discussions of governmental reform and reorganization generally evoke yawns and glazed expressions. That is, government reorganization seems uninteresting until you have to try to work your way through the bureaucratic maze to find out what happened to your delayed Social Security check or how you can participate in a federal housing program. Once you have been referred to your fourth functionary and your problem is still unresolved, your interest in the reform of government will quicken noticeably.

The difficulty in dealing with governments at all

levels results from their phenomenal growth in recent years. The federal government's budget in forty years increased from $3.4 billion in 1930 to $208.1 billion in 1970. Expenditures at the state and local level increased from $9.2 billion in 1932 to $177.5 billion in 1969. In the last ten years alone, federal outlays have more than doubled. Meanwhile state and local government expenditures almost tripled. The 1972 estimated federal budget of $230 billion means that we are spending $7,273 every second of every minute twenty-four hours a day, seven days a week.

The federal payroll has not only increased in Washington, it has spread throughout the country. In California, there are 50 percent more employees of the federal government than there are in Washington, D.C. At last count, 124 separate departments, agencies, bureaus and boards in Washington—and more than 400 regional and area field offices throughout the nation—were providing assistance to states, cities and individuals through over 1,000 separate channels.

This growth at the federal level has often generated chaos. Numerous agencies are either doing the same jobs or working at cross purposes with each other. Nine different federal departments and twenty independent agencies are involved in education. Seven departments and eight agencies work in the field of health. Some cities have as many as twenty to thirty separate manpower programs funded by various federal offices. While the Department of Agriculture pays farmers to drain wetlands, the Interior Department pays to preserve them. The U.S. Forest Service is charged with promoting the conservation and optimum use of our forest land, but it allows lumbering practices which have brought about widespread watershed erosion.

With the ever expanding bureaucracy, the federal government should keep track of its own programs. But it cannot. The proposed federal budget for fiscal 1973, aside from spending $271 billion, fills 1,103 pages. Someone somewhere in the government may have read and understood all 1,103 pages, but he is an exception. It is startling but true that no one really knows how many programs are operated by the federal government. Some estimates run as high as 1,500 separate programs. Senator William Roth of Delaware, while a congressman a few years ago, became incensed about the growth of federal programs and the lack of information. He had a list of hundreds of federal programs compiled to prove that the government was confusing to the people, to the Congress, even to itself. That document is now the best federal program catalog available.

Confusion also reigns in state and local government. Urbanization has made government seem more distant, imposing new, larger forms of government on people as urban and suburban areas grew rapidly and became unmanageable by the old methods. Usually, the old forms of government have been kept as well.

The Committee on Economic Development found a few years ago that a citizen of Fridley, Minnesota, a Minneapolis–St. Paul suburb of 15,000 people, was expected to be an informed elector—that is, vote—for eleven separate superimposed governments, beginning with the federal government and working through the state, the county, metropolitan-wide mosquito abatement and airport authorities and local districts of varying sizes governing soil conservation, hospitals, sanitation, sewers, schools and finally ending up with the city itself.

In the past, Americans said, "You can't fight City Hall," and then gamely waded into the fray anyway, confident of victory or at least a fair fight. Now few people have the will or the resources to try to work through the jungle of government, let alone to fight the New York Port Authority or any of the other mammoth superinstitutions that seem to answer to no one but the dictates of their own computers.

The problem with government today is more than just size and red tape. More and more, people bypass state and local governments and look to Washington for answers to their problems. It is not that they discern greater wisdom housed in the marble buildings of the nation's capital. It is simply that the states and cities are strapped financially and the federal government is the last resort.

The federal government collects 50 percent more from each individual than state and local governments combined. State and local revenues are increasing at a faster pace, but much of these funds come from property and sales taxes, the most regressive forms of taxation. Deficits mount. New York had a deficit of $1.5 billion for fifteen months in 1970 and 1971. California was searching at the end of 1971 for a way of covering a $310 million deficit. The sight of schools closing in cities across our country, once unthinkable, has now become common as municipalities verge on bankruptcy.

Transference of revenue and power to the federal government creates new problems. National solutions are promulgated for regions of the nation that differ markedly. Montana is different from New York. Hartford is unlike Reno. The problems of the states and communities are not the same. Yet the federal bureaucracy too often treats each local situation as if it were cut from the same mold.

The federal government has historically developed

its programs along narrow, well-defined lines. Government regulations require that federal moneys be spent by local governments in a carefully prescribed and categorized manner. Funds are awarded in what have come to be known as "categorical grants-in-aid." They generate as many problems as they solve. First, categorical grants are ridden with red tape. George Romney, Secretary of the Department of Housing and Urban Development, cited a two-and-a-half-foot stack of papers which constituted a single application one city had made for one urban renewal grant.

The proliferation of federal categorical grant programs, each with its own regulations, is confusing beyond belief. Catalogs now have to be published to guide state and local officials through the bewildering inventory of rules and requirements. Inevitably, there is now a catalog of the catalogs.

Even the process of applying for a grant may represent a distortion of local priorities, brought about by the existence of federal funds for some programs and not others. The "gold-plated octagon" example illustrates this phenomenon. One federal official has said, "If the federal government were giving away gold-plated octagons, and the cities had to pay half the cost, every damn city in the nation would have one." Another official said local leaders often complain to him how federal dollars are often available for the wrong projects while no money is offered for what is needed most. "We've got county libraries coming out of our ears," one local official said. "What we really need is a new fire station."

In winning federal funds, states and local jurisdictions effectively tie their own hands because of the "matching funds" principle behind most specific grants-in-aid. The standard procedure in awarding such grants is for a state or city to contribute from 10 percent to 60 percent of the costs from its own funds. A state which is successful at obtaining federal grants soon finds that dollars from Washington severely limit the scope and number of projects which the state can initiate on its own. Aides to Governor William G. Milliken, of Michigan, say that between federal matching funds and other normal fixed requirements, their state budget of $1.95 billion left the governor with real discretion over only $85 million.

A better system must be devised. In 1968 I proposed the establishment of a new Hoover Commission (two earlier commissions, the first headed by former President Hoover, had proposed reorganization plans for the federal government) to study the federal structure and suggest revisions in federal assistance programs and government organization. The Senate passed the bill that year, but the House did not act before adjournment.

Before the new Ninety-first Congress could act, President Nixon appointed an advisory council on reorganization. It was headed by Roy Ash, president of Litton Industries. The council urged streamlining the government into four federal superagencies: departments of Human Resources, Natural Resources, Community Development, and Economic Development. The plan is now before the Congress.

The proposal is a start in the right direction. Unfortunately, it has been drafted and presented in the narrow context of simplifying existing departmental lines. It is reorganization for the sake of reorganization, and that is not good enough. After the desks are moved around and the organization charts redrawn, the true test of reorganization is whether it enables government to deal more effectively with problems and enables us to advance toward achievement of our national goals.

The President's message, for example, stated that the "overriding purpose" of the Department of Community Development would be "to help build a wholesome and safe community environment for every American." This definition of our goals is inadequate. It ignores the problems of urban blight and suburban sprawl. It does not deal with the growing polarization between economic classes, races and residents of the suburbs and central cities. Nor does it provide a plan for balanced growth so that the resources of rural areas can be fully utilized and those of the cities not stretched to the breaking point.

If reorganization is to be successful, we need to know where we are going and how reorganization will help move us there. Otherwise, we may be reorganizing to solve the problems of 1960 or 1970, when we should be looking ahead to 1975 and 1980. We must not waste the present opportunity to restructure our major public institutions by attempting to force the future into the framework of the past.

Reorganization of the executive branch should be accompanied by reorganization of the Congress, since House and Senate committees are structured along agency lines. Committee reorganization on the Hill will require give and take by members jealous of their present prerogatives. We should also streamline the session. Each session should be split into two parts: one legislative, one appropriations. Operating first as lawmaker and then as provider of funds, Congress would avoid the inevitable logjam at the end of each year, when bills pile up awaiting action while the federal agencies await their fate in the appropriations process.

Other procedural reforms are necessary, but the

debate over the filibuster rules in the Senate illustrates the way positions on procedural reform can change. For years, liberals opposed these rules that allow unlimited debate unless two-thirds of the Senate agree to a time limitation. Now some have found that delaying tactics can be useful. They have filibustered against legislation to continue the war in Vietnam, against funding for the supersonic transport (the SST) and against confirmation of conservative-minded Supreme Court nominees. A few liberals have even been candid enough to state that they are reconsidering their positions on this tactic while others claim their "educational" debates are not filibusters at all.

I think filibusters are wrong, no matter what the issue. Senators are legislators, if we are nothing else, and that means we should be willing to vote on an issue after reasonable discussion. To deny the Senate this right is to undercut the very premise upon which the legislative branch is based. Ending the filibuster rule would be an important congressional reform.

The change in attitude—the use of the filibuster by liberals who once opposed it—demonstrates the danger of pursuing procedural changes only in terms of a given issue, be it civil rights or defense spending. Too often the need for reform seems to depend on whose ox is gored. We ought to have a better and more consistent standard by which to judge the validity of suggested reforms.

Any question of reorganization of the federal government raises questions of its relationships to state and local governments. Considerable support has developed to decentralize federal agencies into regional offices. Officials could become more familiar with local problems and more responsive to local constituencies. But decentralization still leaves us with federal officials, not responsible to local citizens, making local decisions. Many would prefer things just that way. Their argument is that local governments are corrupt and inefficient. But often their real feelings are that we at the federal level know better what's good for people than they do themselves.

Critics point out that local and state governments do not often attract the most capable personnel. They assert that performance is poorest at the local level, not much better at the state level and nothing short of brilliant in Washington. That argument, although frequently made, does not tell the whole story. The federal government attracts the people it does because, first, the pay is better in Washington than elsewhere in public service; and second, because the challenge of federal service, at this point in our nation's history, is greater.

Local and state government salaries have not kept

pace with federal pay scales or remained comparable to what private industry pays for similar duties. State and local governments have suffered accordingly. Young men and women just out of college may apply for federal employment and, if they are accepted, can expect a starting income of from $7,300 to $9,000 a year. However, except in states such as California and New York, where salaries are comparable to federal rates, young college graduates often find that state and local government salaries are substantially lower than at the federal level.

Two 1971 studies of state legislatures by the Citizens Conference on State Legislatures revealed that salaries and responsiveness frequently go hand in hand. Legislatures were rated according to their efficiency, accountability, independence and representativeness. The five most effective legislatures, California, New York, Illinois, Florida and Wisconsin also turned out to be among the ten highest paid. In some cases, though, the better-paid legislatures were not as effective as the lower-paid. For example, Massachusetts, sixth in pay, ranked only twenty-ninth in effectiveness, while a relatively low-paid legislature, New Mexico, forty-seventh in pay, was eleventh. Pay, then, is not the only factor. But it is important and cannot be overlooked.

For some people the meaning of the job counts as

much as salary or anything else. Call them idealists, call them people who are looking for action, excitement and a place to put their wit and skills to the test, they are going to seek employment where the challenges are, where they can do the most good. Again the federal government, as of now, has more to offer.

A strong case can be made that the reason some state and local governments seem to be run and staffed by unimaginative and incompetent people is that they have little of consequence to do. All of us have faced moments in our lives when, because of adversity, we performed much better than we thought we could. Conversely, if there is little challenge in our lives, there is, for many, reduced motivation to achieve. In public service, people perform better if they feel what they are doing is important, that it matters that they do a good job. They need to be rewarded financially, of course, but "the meaningful job factor" should never be slighted. Peace Corps and Vista volunteers have shown that money can be a secondary consideration.

What is true of government workers is also true of elected officials. Politicians need challenges beyond the ballot box. If governors and mayors have virtually no power over the major decisions confronting their constituents—if they go to Washington in every crisis—their constituents won't hold them in high esteem. Nor will young imaginative managers and experienced technicians be inspired to join their state administration or team at city hall.

Anyone with a desire to be where the "action" is will tend to gravitate to federal employment—or federal elective office. For them, the idea of public service is synonymous with federal service. That is a tragedy. We as a nation will never be short of lofty goals in Washington. Where America needs idealism the most is in city halls and state capitals.

The place to begin to remedy this situation is with a reallocation of governmental authority at all levels. But we need to recognize that many issues no longer divide up on a strictly "local" or "national" basis. We cannot arbitrarily assign those matters which are "local" in character to state or municipal government and those which are "national" to the federal government. Defense of our country is clearly a national responsibility, and libraries ought to be run locally. But many of America's problems and the solutions they require today are different from those of fifty or a hundred years ago.

Years ago, pollution was considered a purely "local" problem, for example. People could dispose of trash in a variety of ways—burn it, throw it in rivers or lakes or simply dump it on some vacant land. But today burning garbage adds to air pollution, throwing it in lakes and streams fouls valuable waters, and communities all across the country are running out of space for local dumps. New York City's air pollution problem also affects Connecticut and New Jersey. The pollution of Long Island Sound affects the people of New York, Connecticut and Rhode Island.

No single national or local solution exists for pollution and many other problems. There are local problems with national implications, like education, and national problems with local manifestations, like interstate highways. To deal adequately with all of these, we must blend government programs at all levels. Our goal should be coordination in each problem area at the broadest level. Multistate air pollution compacts are needed in some areas while metropolitan-wide housing programs represent coordination at another level. Day-to-day operations and implementation, on the other hand, should be handled at the level closest to the people.

None of this makes any sense if we are going to leave state and local governments so broke they cannot handle their share of these responsibilities. For several years programs of "revenue sharing" have been suggested—that is, returning federal funds to state and local officials to be spent as they see fit. Most "revenue sharing" proposals provide that 1 or 2 percent of federal revenues each year will be given to state and local government for whatever programs they select. President Nixon has also proposed that "special" revenue sharing, or block grants, be developed to consolidate the federal funds already spent in areas such as education and manpower training. Funds would be returned "in block" to state and local government, where the money would have to be spent for programs in the designated area.

Even if these programs are adopted, they will not remove the federal government from the categorical-grant business. Hundreds of programs will remain, and billions of dollars will be spent. There will still be need for an effective reorganization of the federal government. Nor will the figures generally discussed —$15 to 20 billion a year—by themselves significantly change the financial picture for state and local governments now spending $180 billion dollars a year. But they are a start in the right direction.

I support revenue sharing. Opponents of the concept point out that those spending the money will not have to raise it. Therefore they will not be "accountable." I oppose that logic. No one is less accountable than the lower-level civil servant in a regional office administering the day-to-day operation of a federal program. No committee of Congress oversees his work regularly. Only his supervisor passes on his performance, and that supervisor himself is usually well hidden within the bureaucracy. And there is no reason why a federal review and audit cannot ensure that the revenue-sharing funds have been spent for a proper public purpose.

The President has proposed that no categorical requirements or strings be attached to revenue sharing. Few strings should be attached to the projects for which the money will be spent. But there must be requirements that state and local governments be organized to use the money well and exercise their authority responsibly. A legislature that meets only a few days every other year and pays its members a salary of $200 a session will not provide effective government. Reorganization, then, is needed at the state and local level as much as in the federal government and should be a prerequisite for any participation in federal revenue sharing.

Those states and localities which accept revenue sharing should be required to have a legislature that meets every year. State and local taxing resources should be used effectively and revised to insure fairness before revenue-sharing funds are provided. And federal money should not be used simply to replace local funds.

All levels of government need to reform their personnel policies. The Intergovernmental Personnel

Act, passed two years ago, is a start. Under this act, grants are provided to state and local governments to help them improve personnel administrations and employee training. Training programs are needed everywhere. Even a city the size of New York has difficulty continually training and upgrading the skills of its almost 400,000 municipal employees. A survey conducted by the Public Personnel Association showed that only about half the 346 local government personnel agencies covered gave any attention to employee training, and yet training is essential to improve the caliber of employees generally.

In turn, local and state governments should be willing to abolish those agencies and public institutions which have outlived their usefulness. In the late 1940s, I became disenchanted with county governments in Connecticut. By the time I was elected governor in 1954, I was convinced that county government in my own state was unnecessary. Abolishing county government was considered a radical idea when I first proposed it. Gradually, however, the notion began to take hold, as more people came to realize that Connecticut's size, population and governmental structure made county government superfluous. Finally, in 1959, the state legislature approved the proposal. County government was abolished with significant savings to the taxpayers.

I recount my own experience not to recommend ending county jurisdictions elsewhere but to show that the most cherished institutions are often those most in need of reform or termination. We should look at all governmental structures in that frame of mind as we set out to streamline local and state procedures in an effort to bring government back under the control of the governed.

Reforms of government are only half the battle, for the focus of our concern is not the government but the individual. We have seen how his voice has become muted in the halls of government. Individuals are also discovering themselves just as powerless and voiceless as consumers in the market place.

More people are taking their market place complaints to their congressmen and senators. For years, constituent mail generally discussed difficulties citizens were having with government red tape. They found it difficult to get any satisfactory response from a federal agency, and their last resort was a letter to their congressman or senator. My mail from constituents now is increasingly concerned with consumer problems and the relationship of large companies to the individual. Citizens view the companies they deal with—airlines, car makers, drug manufacturers, whatever—as large bureaucracies that are as difficult to penetrate as the government.

To the average person, red tape is red tape. He does not know the name of or have much confidence in the director of consumer relations of a large company like General Electric or the complaint office at the Securities and Exchange Commission. Anyone who has a telephone knows that straightening out an incorrect bill at the phone company is as complicated as deciphering a federal service manual. Confused, perplexed, frustrated, the people write their senators and congressmen.

Congress has the responsibility to get involved, especially where matters of public health and safety are concerned. For example, two weeks before Thanksgiving of 1971, the Government Accounting Office (GAO), the watchdog agency that reports directly to Congress, found that American families were buying and eating poultry that had been slaughtered and packaged in factories crowded with filth and refuse. In a report to my Government Operations Subcommittee, GAO stated it had inspected some sixty-eight plants, approximately one out of every five plants in the nation. The plants inspected produced over a billion and a half pounds of poultry for American kitchens in 1971. Deficiencies were found in every plant. The GAO report maintained that these plants were typical of most poultry factories and slaughterhouses. One plant was described as having areas that "gave the appearance of a cheap horror movie scene." Sanitation was described as "nonexistent." Yet these plants had remained open and continued to process food until this GAO investigation.

Working for higher standards in the poultry and meat industries is a never-ending task under our present system. The federal agency responsible for inspection of poultry and meat plants is the Consumer and Marketing Service of the U.S. Department of Agriculture. In September 1969, I released a GAO report that showed the Agriculture Department had failed to assure decent standards in poultry plants. In June 1970, I released another GAO report that showed that the Department's sanitation standards for meat plants were not being enforced. If we don't change the way we operate, I am confident another similar GAO report can be obtained next year or the year after.

An equally disturbing situation struck even closer to me and my staff recently. Isoniazid is a drug for treating and preventing tuberculosis. Early in 1970 several cases of TB were discovered among workers in cafeterias on Capitol Hill in Washington. The Communicable Disease Center of the Public Health Service responded by undertaking a preventive isoniazid program among congressional employees and others working on the Hill. Skin tests were given.

Those with positive results—in other words, those who had been exposed to TB but had not contracted it—were given isoniazid in 300-milligram tablets. They were not told that very few of those who show positive results on the skin test actually ever come down with TB. Statistics indicate, in fact, that only one of every 1,400 people with a positive reaction actually has or contracts the disease.

The Public Health Service program on Capitol Hill was a disaster. More than twenty persons treated with isoniazid developed hepatitis. One of those was a secretary in my office. Two men, Timothy Bleck, a congressional reporter for the St. Louis *Post-Dispatch,* and Robert Stuckey, a television newsman, died of hepatitis after taking isoniazid. As a result of the diseases and deaths, I asked GAO to investigate the manner in which the 300-milligram isoniazid tablet was developed and administered. GAO found a shocking example of neglect, a total and knowing failure by federal agencies to abide by legal requirements and a permissive attitude about the use of human beings as the subjects for medical experiments.

The GAO found that the Communicable Disease Center had violated federal rules in the testing period for the form of drug used. Then, in administering the drug, the agency did not advise the patients of the known danger of hepatitis. In fact, patients were assured it was "as safe as aspirin."

Other examples fill our papers every day. Mercury in tuna and swordfish, toys dangerous to children or food poisoning—the list is almost endless. In these and scores of other cases, the consumer is helpless to demand better or safer products. Occasionally someone sues and wins a judgment. But companies often view court cases as only a cost of doing business.

A few men like Ralph Nader have demonstrated what dedicated individuals can achieve in making both the government and private enterprise responsive to the legitimate interests of the consumer. But we cannot rely on a few men and women to do the work for all of us, no matter how capable they are. Nor can we ever hope to construct a perfect—or even continually effective—regulatory scheme for every area of concern to the consumer. Regulatory agencies have a tendency to protect the industries they are supposed to regulate. The strongest voices on behalf of regulated industries in Washington often turn out to be the regulators such as the Interstate Commerce Commission, the Federal Communications Commission and the Food and Drug Administration.

Congressional response thus far has been to pass even more consumer protection laws. All of them are needed. Once again, however, proliferation has undercut our programs and made life even more confus-

ing for the consumer. At last count seventy-six consumer programs were spread throughout thirty-four
different departments and agencies.

Obviously these programs should be coordinated.
But more is needed. We need to establish an effective
form of wide-ranging consumer advocacy. It is the
only way the individual will be able to make his voice
heard in the market place. Therefore, my Government Operations Subcommittee has developed a bill
to establish a federal Consumer Protection Agency
as well as a three-member Council of Consumer Advisers in the Executive Office of the President. This
bill passed the Senate late in 1970 before the Congress adjourned. The measure may well be enacted
into law before the end of 1972.

Under this legislation, the Council of Consumer
Advisors will recommend to the President policies to
benefit the consumer and will help coordinate bur-
geoning consumer laws. Of even greater importance,
however, is the independent Consumer Protection
Agency's function of representing the consumer's interest before federal departments, agencies and
courts. Every day the federal government makes decisions or administers programs which affect the
pocketbooks, health and safety of millions of consumers. The regulatory commissions—the Interstate
Commerce, the Federal Trade, the Federal Commu-

nications and the Atomic Energy—are places where the consumer has been unrepresented too often in the past. In license, rate and route hearings, for example, the new Consumer Protection Agency would represent the consumer, actively opposing inflationary price hikes and unjustifiable service cutbacks.

In bringing the interest of consumers to bear on the decision-making processes of government, this legislation merely provides a tool which the business community and other private interests already have at their disposal. Business has its trade associations, vast lobbying operations and a Cabinet department (Commerce) which promotes its interests. Consumers should have the same organization and representation. Although every American is a consumer, each person devotes only a part of his time to his role as a consumer and usually spends a fraction of his money on a given item which may prove unsatisfactory or dangerous. Thus, the buyer has historically been less organized than the seller in the market place and, in turn, has been less represented in the councils of government.

We cannot create the perfect regulatory agency. But we can generate sufficient continuing, independent pressure on these agencies to "encourage" them to act on behalf of the consumer's best interests. If consumers can begin to feel their views are being

heard, and that their views count, we will have begun
to restore some sense of responsibility to the market
place and a greater sense of importance to the lives of
individuals.

VIII

The Economy

THE ISSUES I have discussed thus far—school desegregation, rural and metropolitan development, help for working Americans, welfare reform, enhancement of the individual's role in society—all depend on one thing for success: the performance of the American economy. By economy I mean the way we utilize our resources, how we earn our money and manufacture our products, how we buy, sell and trade our goods and services, what applications we make of technology. If we do these things wisely, progress in all other areas is possible.

But if our economy fails because we do these things poorly, if we make inefficient, thoughtless and shortsighted use of our resources, we will stumble in everything else we set out to achieve. Individual enterprise, imagination and public spirit cannot and will not flourish when there are no jobs, when inflation saps our economic strength, and confidence in tomorrow ebbs, when optimism is in retreat and capital is scarce. The lack of money is the root of much evil.

The American economy is basically the strongest in the world—but it is troubled. More than 5 million of our people are unemployed. Millions more are afraid they may be laid off. Production is stagnating. Our trade balance has tilted against us for the first time since 1893. All over the world, trust in the dollar is at a low point even after devaluation. Yet ours is still the richest, most powerful nation in history. Our technical know-how, the source of much of our economic strength, is still the envy of the world. The majority of our people live better than men, women and children have ever lived. Still, the economic future is uncertain, and so are we.

The doubts that surround the American economy are new. As we started the 1960s, many worried about finding "meaningful" jobs. Now, as we embark upon the seventies, people simply want to find jobs, period. The mid-sixties were fat years. The nation was booming. Unemployment was down. Wages went up. The stock market soared. We could afford the luxury of worrying about the quality of work, for it was assumed that the opportunity for work would always be with us. Now that assumption no longer holds, not for factory workers, not for craftsmen, not for skilled technicians—not even for Ph.D.'s.

In the 1960s, we thought a college degree guaranteed a good job at a good salary. We know better today. In California, for example, the heretofore insatiable demand for teachers has reversed itself, and teachers have become a surplus commodity in the Golden State. Educators have it no worse, though, than those men and women who staked their careers on aerospace. In Seattle, Hartford, St. Louis, Los Angeles—anywhere airplanes and rocket ships are designed and built—engineers and technicians are driving cabs, tending bars and reading the help-wanted ads.

Our economic position abroad is not encouraging, either. The cost of military commitments in Asia and Western Europe has been high. Chronic balance of payments deficits have weakened the dollar. In markets around the world foreign goods replace American goods. America produced nearly half the world's raw steel in 1950. We now produce about 20 percent. Twenty-two years ago America made 76 percent of the world's cars. That has dropped to 31 percent. Consistently first among the world's machine-tool builders year after year, this country is now slipping to fourth behind the Soviet Union, Japan and West Germany. Virtually alone as a leading shipbuilder following World War II, the United States in 1970 built only 2 percent of the tonnage of the world's merchant ships.

Our industries are hurting as even at home we see the relative high cost of manufacturing goods in America. This year more money will be spent buying imports than foreigners will spend buying our exports. Seven of 10 radios are imported from overseas, as are one of every six new cars sold, and more than half of our black-and-white television sets. An American has been described as a person who drives home in a German car from a French movie, slips off his Hong Kong suit and Italian shoes, puts on his English robe and Mexican slippers, and sips Brazilian coffee from Dutch china while sitting on Danish furniture. Then he writes a letter to his congressman on Canadian paper with a Japanese pen—demanding that the government do something about all those foreign imports.

Meanwhile, too much of the industrial and technological capacity of the United States stands idle while the nation is in desperate need of repair and rebuilding. America's lakes, rivers and streams become more and more polluted every year. Our air grows foul. Cities are decaying. Nearly 5 million homes and apartments are substandard. Passenger trains are allowed to fall into disuse and be retired while the need for rapid transit systems is greater than ever. Physically, the country seems to be running down.

Thus, we find ourselves faced with a number of paradoxes. We are rich; yet the dollar has declined in value and monetary stability is not in sight. We have men and women so knowledgeable, innovative and courageous that they can plan and then carry out a trip to the moon and back; yet these same men and women are uncertain of their jobs, if they are employed at all. We have the most advanced technology in the world; yet we cannot mount a successful attack to clean our lakes, purify our air, rebuild our cities or provide public transit for commuters. Our goods are sought and imitated throughout the world; yet we are increasingly buying more foreign products.

How did we get ourselves into this situation? It was easy. We just worried about today and assumed tomorrow would take care of itself. And why not? It always had throughout our history. And so we did not plan ahead. We did not foresee tomorrow's requirements and trends—at home and abroad. Our successful large corporations plan their investments and priorities five, ten and even twenty years in advance. For them, long-term allocation of resources and the assignment of future priorities is a never-ending process. But our own government did not and does not plan ahead. With few exceptions, the U.S. government operates from year to year. The federal budget is essentially a ledger for the next twelve months' operation.

Two exceptions demonstrate the importance of long-range planning. In national defense and space, America made important breakthroughs by awarding long-term contracts and planning ahead systematically on at least a five-year basis. There have been some mistakes. There were bound to be. But over-all the approach has been successful. Unfortunately, it has not been extended to other areas.

In government, comprehensive surveys based on national priorities are rare. Each agency may look ahead on its own. But its projections are necessarily narrow. The Commerce Department foresees its own mission, goals and requirements over the next decade as do the departments of Interior, Labor and Defense. But who is looking at the nation's requirements? Who develops goals for this country on a long-range basis? No one.

We allocate resources, physical and human, on a catch-as-catch-can basis and commit ourselves to the achievement of goals one year that we may lose interest in the next. A case in point is what has happened to the space program.

In 1957, the Soviet Union launched Sputnik I, the first man-made satellite to orbit the earth. In response, we set out on a crusade that pervaded and influenced national policies for the next ten years. We would keep up with and surpass the Russians, and we would educate an entire generation of engineers and scientists to do it.

Young men and women, inspired by the challenge of space exploration—another "new frontier"—and, equally important, assurances that this was, indeed, the field of the future, responded to their nation's sense of crisis. They prepared for careers in space and space-related fields. They became scientists, engineers and technicians in numbers two and three times greater than ever before. The U.S. Office of Education figures show that in 1954–55, men and women receiving bachelor's degrees in engineering totalled 22,589; master's degrees, 4,484; and Ph.D.'s 599. By 1969–70, the numbers had increased to 44,722 B.A.'s; 15,597 M.A.'s; and 3,681 doctorates. Similar rapid increases were registered in mathematics and physics.

Throughout most of this period, the jobs were always there for these people. At the peak of the Apollo Project, 410,000 men and women were working for the National Aeronautics and Space Administration (NASA) in laboratories, assembly lines, launching facilities and universities and colleges. As former NASA Administrator James Webb was fond of saying, America had harnessed the most massive combination of brains and brawn ever assembled in a peaceful pursuit.

Then the bottom fell out. It began in 1968, more than a year before the lunar landing itself. The nation had completed most of the work needed to go to the moon long before astronaut Neil Armstrong took his fateful giant step for mankind. The collapse was not as devastating as the crash of '29. Not as devastating, that is, unless you happened to be one of the more than 250,000 workers, engineers and scientists who have lost their jobs since.

The tragedy of the space program is more than the loss of jobs by thousands of brilliant, dedicated men and women. The tragedy is also that we are now wasting the talents of men and women as well as institutions with the potential for solving some of the most critical problems facing this country. The huge investment in research and development that this country made in support of the lunar landing was not just an investment in space flight. It was an investment in technology. While the return on that money has been substantial—from weather prediction to transoceanic telephone systems and TV transmission —many more new industries could have been born using the funds we put into space research and development.

But no one was planning for new efforts to develop techniques for projects as wide-ranging as solving pollution problems to building rapid transit. NASA was planning ahead—but only in terms of NASA. The space agency came forward with many alternatives, but all of them, quite naturally, called for more NASA, more space exploration, more long-range missions and costly objectives. It wasn't NASA's fault. Space officials are charged with managing America's space program—not setting national goals. But no one in government was looking at the big picture. We should have foreseen, in 1965 and 1966, that a slackening of our space effort was inevitable and that plans were needed to make productive, positive use of the monumental organizational skill and technical competence of the space team.

Even more disturbing, it has now become apparent that our national policy, although never articulated, has been simply that we spend money only for basic research when it applies to war planes and missiles—and not much else. Last year, 79 percent of federally sponsored research was for defense and space. The armed forces, NASA and the Atomic Energy Commission alone have sponsored as much as 60 percent of research and development in industry and the universities as recently as four years ago.

A drop in funding recently has dislocated both industrial and academic efforts to move ahead in science and technology. Scientists are suffering not only in morale but in the pocketbook. The percentage of our gross national product devoted to research and development last year was the lowest since 1960.

Industry, hit with the downturn in the economy and the profit squeeze, is funding less and less research on its own. Research at our leading universities and laboratories has also declined markedly, creating a kind of national research and development depression. A $40 million accelerator, operated jointly by Princeton and the University of Pennsylvania, lost its federal support last year. The program may not continue. At Emory University in Atlanta, federal fund cutbacks threatened basic medical research and behavioral studies. The story is repeated across the country.

So today we have no plans, only vague goals for tomorrow and, ironically, our best hope for the future—our research and skills in high technology—is wasting in the face of economic hardships. Research and development is always the first thing to go in any budget cutback—whether in government or the private sector—and the last to start up again. And yet it is here that we have the possible solution for both our domestic and our foreign economic problems.

Domestically, there is no doubt that we can only make great gains in areas like pollution, mass transportation, health, housing and education if we develop the necessary new technology. Students turning away from research and arguing against further technological gains are, in fact, frustrating our best hope for solving our own as well as the world's social and economic ills.

As C. P. Snow has warned us, "Technology is a queer thing; it brings you great gifts with one hand, and stabs you in the back with the other." The answer is not to run away from technology but to harness it for the purposes we seek to accomplish. The same technology that leads to industrial development and its resulting pollution can help us control that pollution if that becomes one of our goals.

Application of techniques to new problems requires a reshuffling of priorities and leadership willing and able to make long-term policy planning. It also requires a certain vision as well as courage. It was no easy decision for President Kennedy to set as a national goal a lunar landing by the end of the decade of the sixties. It will be even harder when we begin to establish national priorities for the future. But this must be done.

The possibilities of directing high technology to our domestic problems are vast. The list of potential projects includes such intriguing and varied possibilities as cable TV hookups between patients in remote areas and specialists in medical centers, electronic delivery of mail, computerized traffic lights to eliminate rush hour tie-ups, better tools for mining the continental shelf, low-pollution cars, more efficient ways of taking salt out of seawater and recycling of solid wastes. A pilot program is about to start in my state of Connecticut to determine the impact improvements in communication will have upon urban growth. Some predict that picture phones and document transmission over telephone lines will mean that no one will have to go to his office to work. He can work at home and communicate as quickly and as well from there with fellow employees or other business associates. This would substantially alleviate our transportation problem, thereby helping to combat pollution, and would leave people free to live almost anywhere they want.

Simon Ramo, the brilliant scientist and industrialist, has proposed that the President begin our efforts in high technology by what we might regard as a massive pilot program. Following the example of the lunar landing program, we would establish a national goal in conservation, such as cleaning up the Great Lakes by the end of the decade. Much would be gained by such a program. New scientific and engineering advances would be scored. We would know more about cleaning up other lakes more efficiently, with less cost. But technology is not all that is involved. In going to the moon, the uncertainties were few. The only question that mattered was, would the mechanical components of the hardware work? If they worked, the mission had to succeed.

In depolluting the Great Lakes—or cleaning up Long Island Sound or any other body of water surrounded by civilization—the questions are many and more difficult to answer. Cities grew up around the Great Lakes because they were an important and vital avenue for shipping, commerce, industrial production and recreation. In turn, they became a convenient and practical dumping site for city sewage systems and industrial refuse of all kinds.

It is naïve and unrealistic to set goals for the Great Lakes premised on the isolation from the world of commerce and industry and urban needs. The economic growth—indeed, the simple economic survival—of this region rests in large measure on the premise that the Great Lakes will continue to be a waterway of commerce as well as a site for industrial expansion and recreation once again for its inhabitants. The Great Lakes are surrounded by millions of people who must have electrical power, who must have jobs and whose local governments must provide for them efficient and modern sewage and drainage systems. These are the realities we must accept if we are to achieve our goal: Great Lakes that are clean and unpolluted, pure enough to support their natural ecology and yet able at the same time to support a modern civilization.

Going to the moon looks simple in comparison to confronting questions such as: If we stop shipping that causes pollution in the Lakes, how many men and women will be left without jobs? What is the tolerable limit of unemployment we can absorb without losing the support of the very community we are seeking to help? What new industries can be created along the Great Lakes that will provide new job opportunities without fouling their surroundings? How much money is the nation willing to spend to preserve the Great Lakes? What percentage of the national budget will the Congress, with its many competing regional interests, allow to be spent in the Great Lakes? What is a fair allocation of national financial resources?

As Mr. Ramo points out,

> In a sense, then, we will have to regard the whole
> [Great Lakes project] as an experiment, as an at-
> tempt to push forward the frontiers, just as in the
> moon landing program. However, here the project
> will be broader and much more difficult. When
> we speak this time of pushing forward frontiers, we
> mean not only in technology and scientific research
> but also in social and economic relationships and in
> understanding what we can or should do about en-
> vironmental degradation in relationship to broader
> goals of social and economic development of our so-
> ciety.

We will also find that long-range planning is
needed if we are to assemble the resources of the
private economy necessary to approach such a
project. In 1970, in my capacity as chairman of the
Government Operations Subcommittee on Executive
Reorganization, I asked many of the largest defense
and aerospace firms in the United States about con-
verting some of their facilities to domestic production. Many pointed out, correctly, that most of the
areas in which they were expected to convert, such as
pollution, mass transit, low-cost public housing and
education, were areas in which their only likely cus-
tomer was going to be the United States Govern-

ment. They needed more than a one-year or even a five-year commitment before they were going to be able to justify redirecting their present activities.

I was pleased to see that the budget for fiscal year 1973 calls for a 15 percent increase for civilian research and development amounting to $700 million. New emphasis is to be given to developments in the fields of energy, environment, transportation, health, natural disasters and drugs. More significantly, perhaps, the Economic Report of the President talks about two experimental programs which will be initiated to stimulate R&D investments and applications by private firms. There has also been talk recently about a new technologies opportunity program.

This is a welcome start—but it is only that. We still need institutions and concrete programs to transform theories and vague goals into realities. The most appropriate institution to deal with the need for new forms of government-industry cooperation would be a new permanent board which would select areas of national priorities, make long-range plans, and then actually design possible government-industry programs to be funded. As a practical matter, our existing agencies, including the Council of Economic Advisers, are simply too busy on day-to-day problems to be able to do this long-range job properly. Therefore no one is doing it now. In spite of our vast wealth, we have no way of planning for the future of our children.

We must begin to make this sort of planning and commitment at the federal level if we are to mobilize the private sector for our efforts. Once a long-term market is assured, companies will move into these areas. Profits earned from supplying pollution-control equipment or low-cost housing units look just as good on a balance sheet as profits earned from producing sophisticated antimissile systems.

We will also need to recognize that no single company alone will be able to mount the effort necessary to deal with a problem like cleaning up the Great Lakes. Barry Commoner has noted that we must spend more than $40 billion annually on ecological reconstruction alone if our land is to be saved. Money like that and the research and development necessary can come about only through joint efforts and consortia among companies of all sizes.

We need to be willing to revise our antitrust laws as they apply to combinations of companies pursuing public goals. Serious thought should be given in the Congress to modifying our antitrust laws if they are a deterrent to technological progress—so that resources could be pooled for specific ends. It seems obvious that if you want either to rebuild our own devastated inner cities or to build a huge dam in

Africa you need a number of companies working closely together. The application of seventy-year-old antitrust laws to modern-day operations by international consortia clearly puts American companies at great disadvantages. We need workable rules that protect our own citizens from monopolistic trade practices while enabling our corporations to combine to take advantage of changing world markets and the business practices of our foreign competitors. In fact, all of our laws and regulations that inhibit the application of new technology should be scrutinized with an eye to helping rather than hindering.

Recently the automobile companies were found guilty of jointly developing antipollution equipment for automobiles. But the claim here was that they were hindering development of such techniques, not furthering them. What I am talking about is developing programs where companies would be helped in developing new techniques. In that situation, joint efforts should be encouraged, not prohibited. The future should not become the sole domain of those companies large enough to support their own private research and development programs.

The benefits of new federal efforts in areas of high technology such as telecommunications, computers, chemicals and power generators will help solve more than just our domestic problems. Expanded capacity in high technology fields is also our best hope for future strength in world markets. What has often been overlooked in the recent discussions of this country's 2-billion-dollar trade deficit in 1971 is that the United States enjoyed a trade surplus in high-technology products that totaled more than $8 billion. At the same time, we suffered a deficit of $9 billion in nontechnology intensive products.

The reason for our surplus in high-technology goods is clear. While we have the highest level of wages in the world, we also have the most skilled employees and advanced techniques. For example, we use more computers than all the rest of the world combined. In low technological fields—shoe manufacturing, for instance—our skill and technology cannot overcome lower wages abroad. In sophisticated manufacturing areas such as computers, however, our high technology compensates for our higher wages sufficiently to make us competitive.

The signs all point to a continuing U.S. potential for remaining competitive in high-technology exports in the short-term future. Between 1965 and 1970, for instance, computer exports increased from $223 million to $1.1 billion. Machinery went up from $6.9 billion to $11.4 billion. Chemical exports rose from $2.4 billion to $3.8 billion. We can expect these figures to continue to climb—but only if, through renewed investments in research, we can make more sophisticated and imaginative hardware and systems than our trading partners. The slogan of the Japanese Panasonic television and radio people is "just slightly ahead of our time." Our goal has to be to stay "slightly ahead" of Panasonic.

The domestic and international relationships in the development of new forms of high technology can be seen in areas such as pollution control. Depolluting the Great Lakes could generate new technologies and manufactured goods that could be the most marketable and most profitable of all our products. For while the United States is the world's biggest polluter, other industrial nations are increasingly faced with similar problems. The Rhine River in Germany ranks beside any of our polluted rivers for its filth and contamination. Demonstrating its high chemical content, a Dutch newspaper photographer recently took a picture of the Rhine and then developed the raw film in the river's waters. In Italy, many of the once beautiful Mediterranean beaches are scarred with oil, industrial waste and sewage. In Tokyo twenty years ago, Mount Fuji served as a beautiful backdrop for the city. Today, a glimpse of it is rare because of the heavy smog.

Pollution even affects less-developed nations. Seoul, Korea, is said to be the most air-polluted city of all. In fact, smog and industrial-waste-laden rivers have become a kind of status symbol to the have-not countries. Pollution signals their economic emergence. They don't like it. But they would rather be polluted than poor. They, as well as the developed nations, constitute a market for American antipollution equipment. They cannot afford the needed research and experimentation to develop these techniques themselves. But they will be prepared, sooner or later, to buy the finished product. Similar markets could exist for urban transit systems, housing, health-care equipment and other hardware and systems enabling nations and communities to solve the physical problems of industrialization and urbanization.

The necessary government support for the research and development to make these programs real will have to be founded on a recognition of the importance of world trade in the future to our domestic economy. Unfortunately, we have only recently become concerned about world trade and investment problems as a nation. Perhaps because our foreign trade accounts for only 4 percent of our gross national product—or because we mistakenly view ourselves as the economic center of the world—our national leaders have tended to neglect international economic issues as they designed and implemented our foreign policy.

The leaders of other industrialized nations see things differently. They give a top priority to foreign trade and investment. The countries of Europe, relying on trade as a source of from 20 to 40 percent of their gross national products, consider foreign sales an essential aspect of foreign policy, and act accordingly. While we occupied ourselves with maintaining military alliances and force levels during the last twenty years, our friends—even those we were so anxious to defend—went on to other things. While the United States concerned itself with the NATO order of battle, West Germany was concerned with filling orders for Volkswagens.

Just how out of step we are in world economic affairs was demonstrated vividly to me in January 1970, June 1971 and January 1972, when, as chairman of the Senate Finance Subcommittee on International Trade, I traveled to Europe to confer with foreign economists, bankers, industrialists and government officials. It became obvious that these people mean to sell their products to anybody who will buy them. Ideological and political considerations concern them little, if at all. Absent from their casual conversations and their formal discussions were references to the cold war, military treaties, pacts and the iron curtain. To paraphrase President Calvin Coolidge, the business of Europe is business.

In Rumania and Hungary, for example, I was impressed by serious efforts to make economic progress and by the desire of top national leaders to increase their commercial ties with the West, particularly the United States. These countries especially admired American technological achievement. On several evenings I met informally with groups of Hungarian and Rumanian university students, the hand-picked future elite of their countries. Most of their questions dealt not with the SALT talks or with the détente in Europe or even with the war in Asia— but with the high American standard of living and how we achieved it. They wanted to learn about American technical competence and what applications the U.S. was making of its resources.

Daily in Eastern Europe I saw French, German, Italian and British businessmen scurrying around with bulging briefcases. These were salesmen—high-level, perhaps, but still salesmen—and they were enthusiastic about the trade opportunities open to them as Eastern Europe becomes more and more a market for them. I wondered where the American businessmen were. I didn't see many. American involvement in total free world trade with East Europe and the Soviet Union comes to a scanty 3 percent. Yet, even then—small as our trade is with these countries— America enjoys almost a 2 to 1 export advantage and, in 1971, a healthy $175 million surplus.

We could do much more if we tried. It has been estimated conservatively that once our trade restrictions were eased with Eastern Europe and the Soviet Union, United States trade with these nations could reach $2 billion by 1975, or, according to more optimistic estimates, as much as $5 billion.

Opportunity, then, awaits us in Eastern Europe if we only begin to develop it. American exports to Eastern Europe can increase more than tenfold, bringing profits to our businesses and wages and new job opportunities to workers. Eastern Europeans, as well as their Soviet neighbors, want desperately to modernize their countries. They know better than we ourselves appreciate that when shopping for the instruments of modernization, it is best to shop first in America. Unfortunately, high tariffs and lack of commercial credit prevent Eastern Europeans and Russians from getting in the front door. As long as our sales to these countries do not have direct military or strategic applications, I say sell them anything they want to buy. Our allies—the Germans, the Japanese, the French, the Canadians—are doing it. Why shouldn't we?

Regrettably, American policy in Eastern Europe, Russia and elsewhere overseas is still dominated by a World-War-II-era thinking. Most of our leaders today learned their foreign policy at a time when giants like Roosevelt, Churchill, Stalin, de Gaulle and Hitler strode across the stage of history, seeking to respond to their people's needs in an often intensely personal manner. Those days are gone. That style is behind us. The world has not seen the last of great men, I hope. But the issues have changed. The romance has been taken out of militarism. The political giants have been replaced by teams of managers, salesmen and technicians. A nation's historic destiny does not concern most people as much any more. "Geopolitics"—military pacts, treaties and balance of power diplomacy—is being replaced by "ecopolitics"—developing international trade and investment policies to achieve economic prosperity and a higher standard of living.

To see ecopolitics in action today, we need look only as far as the two principal antagonists of the Allied cause in World War II. The Germans and the Japanese are introducing methods and processes more advanced than ours in some of the basic industries where we once dominated the field. The Japanese are exercising a remarkable foresight in adapting to changing circumstances. If they find, for example, that, for one reason or another, they cannot compete in an industry where they once were strong, they simply phase out production and go on to something else where they can compete.

One illustration of the Japanese adaptability is in the textile industry. Japan, whose rapid growth in exports helped cripple the American textile industry, found in the late sixties that it could not compete with cheaper textiles from Hong Kong, Korea and Taiwan. The Japanese responded to this by allowing their textile production to decline accordingly, putting new stress instead on other industries where they felt they could compete. They concentrated on their steel industry, for instance. The investment paid off handsomely. In the next few years Japan will not only be the most technologically advanced and most efficient steel producer in the world; it will also be the largest.

The lesson for America in all this is that we should concentrate our efforts in those areas where we can hope to achieve a superior competitive position. Unfortunately, we aren't doing this on a systematic basis. Western Europe and Japan are racing ahead on research and development in new industrial techniques, in plant modernization and marketing analyses. They are pulling alongside of us and even ahead in areas we once could legitimately call our own. They are making these advances by pooling their resources, by calling upon the best minds in their governments, industries and universities.

We should be doing the same thing, but we are not. The federal government is not doing enough to assist American businesses expand and develop new markets abroad. This assertion is contrary to the widely held belief that this country's foreign policy is heavily influenced by business interests and is really nothing other than "economic imperialism." At some earlier stage in our history there may have been examples of this, notably with our attempts to influence Latin and South America on behalf of companies like Standard Oil and United Fruit. But that is history, and those shouting about economic imperialism are flogging a dying, if not already dead, horse.

The truth of the matter is that U.S. government officials and American businessmen do not work together to any significant degree in the pursuit of foreign trade objectives. American business leaders have less influence on governmental decisions and receive less help from their government than do their counterparts in any other industrial nation. In Japan, for instance, close collaboration exists between government, industry, banks and labor when it comes to foreign commerce. In Western Europe, governments also work diligently to promote the interests of their business enterprises.

Conversely, our government is not organized to strengthen American business interests overseas.

With some sixty federal agencies involved in various aspects of foreign trade policy, it is unbelievably difficult for an American corporation to find out where to petition for assistance and guidance.

I have already talked about the need for joint, long-range planning by government and industry if we are to succeed in applying our technological skills to solving many of our domestic problems. The same joint effort needs to be made on the international level, where many of those same new products will find major new markets. The establishment of a White House Council on International Economic Policy last year was a beginning in the right direction, but it is only a first step. We need ongoing planning and analyses about the foreign markets of the future if we are to avoid losing our place in world trade and investment entirely.

Developing greater production and sales of high-technology goods, of course, is not the total answer to our economic and trade problems. It will take us years to transfer more of our resources into these fields, and the threats to our economy won't wait that long. Andrew Biemiller, director of the AFL-CIO Washington office, estimates that foreign competition cost American workers approximately 700,000 jobs between 1966 and 1969. The chairman of the Zenith Radio Corporation, Joseph S. Wright, who

testified before my subcommittee, believes that
47,000 jobs have been lost to imports in the electronics industry between 1966 and 1970. The American
Footwear Manufacturers Association's estimates are
that imported footwear products have wiped out
76,250 job opportunities and that the figure could
reach 169,200 by 1975. While these figures are dis-
puted by those who argue that growth in import- and
export-related industries makes up the slack, there is
a real problem—at least for some of our biggest industries.

The question is what do we do for these workers in
the two decades we are transferring into high technology? Economists and theoreticians talk about the
shifting of resources and long-run adjustments. But
as the economist Keynes noted, in the long run, we're
all dead. In the meantime, what does a senator tell a
fifty-year-old workman who loses his job after twenty-
one years because his employer, the Royal Typewriter Company, moves from Hartford to Hull, England? That happened in 1971, and some 2,000 men
and women will lose their jobs before it's all over.
These are workers with families and mortgages and,
at the moment, cheerless futures, particularly the
older men and women. Do I recite to them the economic theory of comparative advantage, pointing out
that they are free to work elsewhere while our indus-

tries adjust to the new competition? Granted, the American people are the most mobile in the world. But how do you tell a middle-aged draftsman who has lived in Hartford all his life to pull up stakes and move his family to Phoenix, then perhaps to California, and finally to Alaska?

American elected officials are not the only people who are confronted with such difficult problems on the issue of trade. Other nations' leaders face similar problems. The recent pronouncement of French President Georges Pompidou comes to mind. Concerned that the European Common Market might relax its strict controls on agricultural imports hurting his own country's farming industry, President Pompidou said, "French farmers can count on my interest in them and on my obstinacy." I can understand President Pompidou's concern, and I have no quarrel with it. For when push comes to shove, every nation and every leader is going to be concerned about the welfare of his people. And until we formulate an international trade policy that recognizes this fact, we will continue to operate in a world of delusions.

For years the United States was preeminent in world trade, and we could set whatever rules we wanted. The only question was how magnanimous we would be. When events so moved us, we were generous with our wealth, as demonstrated by the assistance we provided for the economic recovery of the world's devastated industrial nations after World War II.

But times have changed. No longer are we Snow White on center stage surrounded by the Seven Dwarfs. Inclusion of Britain, Denmark, Norway and Ireland in the Common Market has created an economic entity with a population of 250 million, a gross national product equal to 75 percent of ours and four times our reserves of gold. This new union is capable of dealing head to head with any other country or economic bloc.

The President's announcement of his new economic policies on August 15, 1971, dramatized how long this country had permitted its trade and economic position in the world to slide. The imposition of a 10 percent surcharge, the untying of the dollar from gold, and, four months later, an official devaluation of the dollar were admissions that patchwork solutions to the world's money and trade problems were no longer sufficient. These actions underlined the sad fact that we have no coherent foreign economic policy.

We have also found that the old shibboleths of "free trade" and "protectionism" no longer make much sense. We need a foreign trade policy that consists of more than a few slogans. Nobody wants a trade war. Everybody wants to trade freely with foreign countries. As a nation, we want to be fair in our dealings with others. We have shown many times that we can be generous with our wealth. But, conversely, we want our country to prosper economically, and we want to be able to compete on fair terms. We cannot be expected to stand by and smile graciously while our trading partners keep American products and firms out of their markets, threaten the vitality of our major industries and weaken this economy already limping along with heavy unemployment. We may think the world of our friends across the seas, but charity begins at home. Like all other nations, we must base our world trade policies on the principle of mutual self-interest.

What we need is a dual-track system for expanding world trade that coordinates imports and exports to prevent any shattering effect on a particular economy or group of workers. We are talking about a problem that has been germinating for years and will require the individual and collective wisdom and judgment of the leaders of the industrialized world to solve. For it will take twenty years to fold Mr. Pompidou's farmers into the French economy so that the people of France can buy cheaper food from Canada and the United States. And it will take years to replace a plant like the Royal Typewriter plant in Hartford.

Neither Mr. Pompidou's farmer nor the typewriter maker in Hartford should be dumped suddenly into unemployment and poverty to further an economic model. The task is formidable, and the journey will be long and tedious, but there is no other way.

A beginning can be made here and in other countries through new, expanded forms of adjustment assistance for workers and industries beginning to lose their ability to compete with foreign imports. No company wants to talk about making adjustments for any phased withdrawal from one market and development of another, but necessity alone will do wonders, as seen by the rapid diversification of tobacco companies into other fields once the Surgeon General's report on smoking and health was published.

Adjustment assistance for both companies and workers was provided for in the 1962 Trade Expansion Act. But ten years after these laws were placed in the books, the actual record of accomplishment is dismal. Some 20,000 workers have been helped temporarily, and only two companies, a shoe manufacturer and a barber-chair producer, have received any substantial assistance from the government. One piano manufacturer in New York who sought adjustment assistance claimed that every time he sent Department of Commerce officials another batch of figures to prove that his company had been injured by imports, they asked for more figures. If any company going out of business had to wait this long—they'd certainly be out of business.

Adjustment assistance as it was conceived ten years ago was obsolescent the day it was enacted. Its requirement of strict proof of a direct relationship between injury due to tariff reductions and imminent financial ruin is virtually tantamount to requiring bankruptcy before providing any help. The emphasis must now be put on spotting in advance those industries and companies in the economy which are running into trouble. Retraining programs should be offered to workers and loans for retooling made available to companies. We should concentrate on helping workers and advising management before the company fails. Unless we do this, the government will always be in a position of doing too little, too late—and the pressures for quotas and other forms of protection will become irresistible.

We should also recognize that no President and no Congress is going to allow the basic industries of our economy to weaken or be destroyed. Industries such as steel, chemicals, autos and electronics, no matter how compelling the economic theory, are not going to be phased out. But these industries have no right to absolute protection for inefficiency. Incentives and assistance should be provided to ensure that in these basic areas we are as modern and efficient as any nation.

New policies will also have to come to grips with the rise of a new force in international affairs: the multinational corporations. No one nation claims them. They, in turn, claim no nation. The world is their home. Not since the great conflict between church and state throughout Europe has there been such a challenge to the sovereign power of individual nations.

Multinational corporations like Shell and Unilever have existed for years. But in the past decade their growth has been phenomenal. These companies now create one-sixth of the world's gross product, and it is estimated that, within thirty years, they will control half of the world's total output. Only a small percentage of companies around the world are involved. Every large company is not multinational, but sixty-two of the top one hundred American companies have production facilities in at least six foreign countries. Multinational companies often are the strongest firms. Well-known economic powers like General Motors, IBM, Standard Oil, Ford, General Electric and Litton Industries highlight the roster.

Multinational corporations link their plants in different countries as if they were manufacturing a single product on several assembly lines in a single factory. The Massey-Ferguson Corporation, for example, makes tractors in the United States for sale in Canada that contain British-made engines, French transmissions and Mexican axles.

Multinational corporations often produce sophisticated goods and machinery for which management, capital and technology have become more significant than labor. Relatively skilled labor exists in many countries. Since the transfer of management, capital and technology across national borders is easy, companies can shift facilities with little concern about labor.

The increasing size and flexibility of these companies have allowed them to begin to dictate terms to nations as well as other companies. The assets of General Motors, for instance, are larger than the gross national products of most of the countries in the world, including nations such as Indonesia and Austria. Henry Ford recently told Prime Minister Heath of England very bluntly that if the government did not improve its labor situation, Ford would simply transfer production to another country. Operating across national borders, these companies are usually in a position to answer only to themselves and their stockholders.

We must develop a system to encourage or require multinational corporations to recognize the great social responsibilities they have as a result of the enormous economic powers they have to ruin communities or entire countries.

Consider the decision by Litton Industries to transfer their typewriter production from Hartford to Hull, England, a situation that has confronted other communities across this country. In Europe, multinationals feel a responsibility to maintain employment when particular industries are displaced by outside competition. Workers are transferred to jobs in the same city, or another production facility is brought in to supply them with jobs in an effort to alleviate the hardship. No multinational corporation in Europe would do what Litton did in Hartford. No corporation should be allowed to do so in the future if it is to be permitted freely to transfer capital, technology and management skills throughout the world.

The Congress, the President and the world community are only beginning to scratch the surface of these problems. Years of work lie ahead. Multinational operations, technological growth and economic interdependence represent unchartered territories.

To succeed in the future, the United States must develop new mechanisms to stimulate our economy, promote technological progress, and manage our relations with the rest of the world. We must begin to establish objectives in terms of our national needs for the next few decades, and not merely the political needs of the next few years. The active cooperation of all—including our universities, industry, labor and the Congress—are needed if we are going to maximize our resources for the benefit of all mankind.

I am confident that America can meet this challenge.

Conclusion

THE PROBLEMS DISCUSSED in this book, while limited in number, span our nation. All of us are affected by them, and the future of our country is tied to how we resolve them.

At many points I have criticized our present policies, warned against the directions we are headed in the future, and suggested solutions. Much needs to be done, but I remain optimistic that we will generate the national will necessary to move ahead.

Many disagree and argue that we are a nation on the way to repeating Rome's decline and fall. They cite the heated social conflicts in America as proof that the worst is yet to come. I think they are wrong.

Great social change is never accomplished without some discord. The present is no exception, and change is already taking place. The very fact that so many Americans are concerned about our status represents a step forward. Without widespread public acknowledgment of the seriousness of current and impending conditions, any real response by a society to its problems is impossible.

But more than concern surrounds us. The beginning of progress can be seen as well. Students are now on university boards of trustees; minority groups, women and young people will be substantially represented at the 1972 Democratic convention; blacks are making some economic progress and appear on television shows, in national advertising and in some of the most traditional law firms; women are being taken seriously as individuals for perhaps the first time; public outcry dismissed a President and is ending a war; weapons systems and the SST are subject not only to greater criticism but sometimes to defeat; and parents have stopped shouting at their children and are beginning to listen to them in an effort to understand what they're trying to say.

These actions are only a beginning, but they represent a recognition by many that people must learn to interact more constructively with one another. America's most important resource is not national wealth or even superior technology. This is a great nation because of the joint efforts of a great people, united by shared hopes and aspirations.

Many people today are trying to withdraw into their own separate worlds. Their vision is limited to how things affect them immediately—not how they affect the country. But if our country fails, we all fail.

In earlier times of crisis in American history, the nation survived because the people rallied behind their government. "We must all hang together," Benjamin Franklin said in that famous speech two hundred years ago, "or assuredly we shall all hang separately." It was good advice then. It is good advice now. It is, in fact, our best hope.

We may not all be of the same origin, or have the same beliefs on all issues. But those qualities of spirit that unite us are more important than those that divide us. All of us, rich and poor, black and white, young and old want the same things for ourselves and for our children: respect as individuals, not treatment as members of a stereotyped class, freedom from discrimination of any kind and the opportunity to reach the upper limit of our abilities. A country with our basic philosophy, great resources and varied experience should be able to meet these aspirations.

Too often we have set idealistic goals and failed to continue the commitment needed to achieve them. Our challenge today is to bring together idealism and workable solutions to our problems. I believe we can do it. If so, America can make it.

SENATOR ABRAHAM RIBICOFF

ABRAHAM RIBICOFF was born on April 9, 1910, in New Britain, Connecticut. He attended New York University and the University of Chicago Law School where he received his law degree, graduating *cum laude* in 1933. After practicing law in Hartford, Connecticut, he was elected to the Connecticut General Assembly in 1938 and was reelected in 1940. In 1942 he was appointed municipal judge in Hartford, a position he held until 1948 when he was elected to the U. S. House of Representatives. In 1954, after two terms as congressman, he was elected governor of Connecticut.

The first political figure to publicly urge Senator John F. Kennedy to seek the Presidency, he was Kennedy's first Cabinet appointee, as Secretary of Health, Education and Welfare. In 1962, he was elected senator from Connecticut, and was reelected for a second term in 1968.

Senator Ribicoff has served in public life for 33 of his 61 years, and is the only active American public official to have held office as a member of the state legislature, a municipal judge, a member of Congress, governor, Cabinet officer and U. S. Senator.

He has received honorary degrees from 24 colleges and universities. He is married and has two children and four grandchildren.